Smash and Grab

SMASH AND GRAB

Robert Murphy

**Gangsters in the
London Underworld 1920-60**

ff

faber and faber
LONDON · BOSTON

First published in 1993
by Faber and Faber Limited
3 Queen Square London WC1N 3AU

Typeset by Datix International Limited, Bungay, Suffolk
Printed in England by Clays Ltd, St Ives plc

A CIP record for this book is available from the British Library

ISBN 0-571-15442-5

2 4 6 8 10 9 7 5 3 1

for Anne

Contents

Preface

My interest in the murky history of the English underworld developed when I was writing an article about the 'spiv' films of the forties. I discovered the reality they touched upon was at least as interesting as the films themselves, and was able to delve deeper when I was commissioned to write a television drama research document about the rivalry between fifties underworld bosses Jack Spot and Billy Hill. I would like to thank Jack Spot, Stan Jaanus and Eddie Chapman, along with several other people who might prefer to remain nameless, for the trouble they took to guide my investigations, and Tracey Scoffield, Clare Noel and Michael Jackson for their support and inspiration. I regret that my interpretation of events is unlikely to satisfy anyone entirely. Truth is an elusive concept in the underworld and the most plausible and convincing stories are often mutually contradictory.

The origins of my book have left their mark on the way in which it is organized. The first six chapters deal with crime between the wars, beginning on the fringes of the underworld – night-life, drugs, prostitution – and moving on to the racetrack protection gangs and the activities of burglars, safe-breakers and smash-and-grab raiders. I have also included what I hope is a sympathetic account of the police, the men who, for low salaries and long hours, attempted to hold in check the wave of crime. Chapters 5 and 6 deal at some length with the obverse to the colourful, exciting life of the successful criminal on the loose – the grim, brutalizing routine of the prison.

The first half of the book does push forward a number of characters – the night-club queen Kate Meyrick, the country house cracksman 'Gentleman George' Smithson, the drug dealer 'Brilliant' Chang, the racing gangster Darby Sabini, the safe-breaker Eddie Chapman, and smash and grab raiders Ruby Sparks and the 'Bobbed-Haired Bandit'. But I thought it was more important to map out the hidden history of the underworld during this period than to dwell in detail on their personal lives. The second half of the book concentrates more narrowly on two major figures, Jack Spot and Billy Hill, rival claimants to the title of 'Boss of Britain's Underworld' in the fifties.

Underworld history and mythology have tended to take Hill's part. He was the victor in the struggle for power in the mid-fifties and he continued to command the respect of later underworld celebrities such as the Kray brothers and the Great Train Robbers. After 1956 Spot disappeared into obscurity, and in contrast to the cleverly written biography of Hill ghosted by celebrated crime journalist Duncan Webb, he had only the lurid fiction of Hank Janson's *Jack Spot: The Man of a Thousand*

Cuts to represent his side of the story. Spot is no paragon of honesty and integrity, but his account of events, told to me over several hours of interviews, is rooted in the brute realities of underworld life rather than in the persuasive imaginings of a crime reporter trying to make acceptable the life of a major criminal. I cannot share Spot's view of himself as a Robin Hood of the East End, but the fact that he was a Jewish strong-arm man in a period of anti-semitic violence does give a certain dignity to his illicit activities.

This is by no means an insider's view of the underworld. Even in my misspent youth, my own criminal activities hardly went beyond smoking the odd joint and walking out of Foyles with an unpaid-for book. Among the sharp, wily people of the underworld I would be instantly recognized as a mug – bad at concealing my motives, incapable of thinking ahead, untidy and sometimes incoherent, the sort of person turned away from both respectable and unrespectable night-clubs. But opposites sometimes attract and, without wishing to glamorize the underworld artificially, I want to do justice to a number of men who, for a variety of reasons, rebelled against society and chose a colourful but not particularly profitable way of life in which courage, endurance, ingenuity and a degree of recklessness were essential for survival. As the Communist Wilfred Macartney, who served eight years in Parkhurst for a bungled act of subversion in 1927, put it: 'It may be fancied that I am making heroes out of men whom society has deemed reprehensible, but I am concerned only with the behaviour of certain men in adversity. Whether it be their own fault or whether it be the fault of society it is idle to argue.'

Robert Murphy, Sheffield, January 1992

INTRODUCTION: UNDERWORLD ETHICS

The robber is a tradesman who, from economic or other pressures, chooses a trade with greater rewards and dangers than navvying ... They are extravagant, addicted to boasting, often impatient of conventional morality. When they have pulled off a big job they celebrate expensively, laugh defiance of danger past, scorn hypothetical dangers to come. They tend to herd together with their own kind, and despise mugs. They develop an intimate jargon of their own, are suspicious of, or hostile to, untried new-comers, respectful towards the aces ...

Jim Phelan, *Jail Journey* (1940)

Criminal traditions

The underworld in Britain is more secretive and less glamorous than it is in America. Except for the Kray brothers' brief dalliance in the limelight, British gangsters have operated so unobtrusively that they have sometimes seemed invisible. Not that they have always shunned publicity. Much of the evidence I have used for this story is dredged from biographies and autobiographies of crooks and policemen. Such books often reached a wide readership but they passed rapidly into oblivion and their testimony has been forgotten.

The British underworld rarely indulged in the spectacular gun battles which gave Prohibition America its cinematic appeal. British gangsters relied on chains and coshes and easily discarded beer bottles when giving battle. Enemies and traitors were not machine-gunned from cars but visited by the chiv-man, who would carefully slice a face with his taped-down razor or chop through collar bones with his little hatchet. Strict censorship against the portrayal of real-life crime prevented ritualistic punishments such as these being shown in British films, and there are only yellowing press cuttings to remind us of the more spectacular eruptions of the pre-Kray underworld – Darby Sabini's takeover of the racecourse rackets, the society scandals caused by the drug dealings of 'Brilliant' Chang, the smash-and-grab exploits of Ruby Sparks and the 'Bobbed-Haired Bandit', the Dartmoor Mutiny of 1932, and the struggle for power between rival 'bosses of the underworld' Jack Spot and Billy Hill.

There is a popular misconception that the period between the demise of the Victorian underworld and the rise of the flashy, brutal gangsters of the sixties was a golden age when deferential bobbies walked their beats and burglars wore striped jerseys and carried sacks of swag. True, there was a gradual taming of the overcrowded, under-policed Victorian cities, but at the same time a huge illegal gambling industry grew up and there were significant technological advances in safe-breaking and armed robbery. These developments encouraged the emergence of British gangsters whose power and influence extended far beyond that of their Victorian forebears – Billy Kimber, Darby Sabini, Alf White, and finally Jack Spot and Billy Hill.

In the nineteenth century the traditional criminal areas of London were ruthlessly uprooted. The rookeries of St Giles and Clerkenwell, 'ancient citadels of crime and vice', were destroyed when New Oxford Street, Queen Victoria Street and Farringdon Street were driven through them in the 1840s and 1850s. Other black spots like the Nichol, a ghetto off Bethnal Green Road made famous by Arthur Morrison's novel *A Child of the Jago*, were wiped out in the slum clearance schemes of the late nineteenth century. Gareth Stedman Jones, plotting the progress of 'Outcast London', found that by the early years of the twentieth century, 'Large and packed residential areas had given way to acres of warehouses, workshops, railway yards, and offices,' and that 'an extensive no-man's land of offices, government buildings, railway yards, warehouses and wharves insulated upper-class from working-class London.'

The break-up of the old criminal communities allowed a clearer line to be drawn between the labouring classes and the dangerous classes. The underworld became a smaller, more exclusive society in the interwar years, and there was less intermingling between 'steamers' (steam-tug = mug) living honest lives and 'wide people' who didn't. The unemployed of Victorian society combined casual labour with petty crime. The unemployed of the twenties and thirties were more likely to be skilled workers – shipbuilders, miners, steelworkers, spinners and weavers – living in respectable communities whose 'criminal activities' hardly extended beyond picking coal from slag heaps or finding ways to avoid having their means-tested unemployment benefit cut. At the other end of the social scale, as aristocratic interest in prize fights and drunken revelries gave way to more refined pastimes, the need for involvement in the underworld ceased. Only on the racetracks did a whiff of nineteenth-century raffishness linger on.

In the early years of the twentieth century there was an alarming growth in the use of firearms. Russian anarchists settled in the East End of London failed to differentiate between armed Tsarist police and the much less ferocious English bobby, and the Siege of Sidney Street in 1911, where a group of cornered anarchists with firearms had to be flushed out by the Scots Guards, provided an eye-opening example to English villains. The troubles in Ireland and the First World War made guns easily available and East End villains like Arthur Harding and Ikey Bogarde used Mauser pistols and heavy Royal Ulster Constabulary revolvers in their internecine conflicts. But firearms didn't really suit the tempo of English and Scottish underworld life and by the twenties most London and Glasgow villains had reverted to using broken glasses and bottles. Sir Percy Sillitoe, the policeman responsible for smashing the Sheffield gangs in the twenties and the Glasgow gangs in the thirties, recalled:

Their favourite weapon in a skirmish was a beer bottle. This had several advantages over other weapons. If you carried a gun or knife it was troublesome to be found in possession of it, but a beer bottle could be carried legitimately. It was handy to use as a club, and could be smashed and used devastatingly with its jagged, newly broken edges, to scalp or disfigure an opponent. In a retreat, or when the enemy fled from close combat, it was an inexpensive missile.

For many people life between the wars was harsh and impoverished. Until they were destroyed by Hitler's bombs, there were still London streets, such as Campbell Road near Finsbury Park, Edward Square and Bemerton Street in Islington, Wilmer Gardens and Essex Street in Hoxton, and parts of Notting Dale, which were virtually no-go areas as far as the police were concerned, and the 'rough house' ethos still ruled in the slum areas of the northern industrial cities. Sir Robert Mark, who became Commissioner of the Metropolitan Police in 1972, recalled that, when he was a constable in Manchester in the thirties, street battles took place between police and locals where uniformed and plainclothes men cheerfully joined in and 'a good time was had by all', both sides taking in good part smashed heads and broken limbs.

Brute force remained a very tangible asset and during the twenties and thirties East End villains like Dodger Mullins. Jimmy Spinks, Wassle Newman, Timmy Hayes and Jew Jack the Chopper King acquired fearsome reputations for their reckless violence. Newman would go into a pub and take a man's beer away, daring him to protest. He was reputed to toss bricks up in the air and punch them as they came down to toughen his fists, so nobody who knew him took up the challenge. Mullins, tiring of a demanding girlfriend, pushed her out of a moving car and broke her back. Spinks, enraged at being asked to pay for his fish and chips, threw the chip shop cat into the fryer. Jimmy Dalziel ('Razzle Dazzle'), leader of a thirties Glasgow gang, the Parlour Boys, would dance with one of his henchmen rather than reveal any vestige of softness by dancing with a girl. And Arthur Skurry, one of whose ears had been bitten off in a fight, refused to exchange his cap and choker for a smart suit for fear his gang of Upton Park gypsies would think he'd become a 'poof'.

By the forties, as the underworld began to follow the example – in dress if not in the use of firearms – of the American gangster film, such attitudes came to be considered old-fashioned. Eddie Raimo, hit man for the King's Cross gang, adopted George Raft's black shirt and white tie and affected an American accent; 'Carl Brisson', a Leeds coalman and leading protection racketeer during the Second World War, borrowed his name and style of dress from the Danish boxer who starred in Hitchcock's *The Ring* and then went on to Hollywood. But Jack Spot and other tough guys continued to use Dettol rather than 'scent' as their aftershave and underworld mores remained substantially unchanged.

Mark Benney (Henry Ernest Degras), growing up in the twenties with a wild, hard-drinking mother on the fringes of the underworld, learnt that there were but two classes of people:

the Wide people, and the Mugs, who exist solely to be fleeced by the Wide people. The Mugs are respectable, honest, hard-working, moderate-living, dull, church-going, fundamentally stupid and credulous. The Wide people are totally indifferent to the virtues defined and possessed by the Mug-majority. They live gaily, love promiscuously, drink vastly, sing loudly, lie brazenly, swagger outrageously and hate dangerously. Above all they never work.

Jim Phelan, an Irish gunman who served thirteen and a half years of a life sentence in English prisons, pours scorn on the press interpretation of a 'wide boy' as a thick-set, flashily dressed thug in a padded-shouldered suit. He argues that 'wide' or 'wa-eed' is actually Arab/Gypsy *ouaide*, meaning outlaw, and that the wide people were a cohesive fraternity with their own private signs and language (a mixture of backslang, rhyming slang, thieves' cant, fairground slang and Romanes) which had its own clearly defined morality.

Phelan, a prolific and talented story-teller, writes with the zeal of a convert in the numerous books he authored after emerging from Parkhurst in 1937. They are an invaluable corrective to books written from a conventional law and order standpoint, but his upright, perceptive, good-hearted criminal heroes are not entirely representative. Benney, who came to realize that the glamour of the underworld concealed an awful lot of sadness and cruelty, was more sceptical, but the ideal of the wide man retained a lingering allure for him:

The wide man must, first and foremost, have a deep indifference to the prevailing economic, social, and sexual conventions of the day. He must not work in the conventional way for his upkeep and he must have a tolerant contempt for those who do . . . His cunning and his luck are what he relies on to give him his fill of the good things of life; and whatever he acquires by these means must be spent extravagantly . . . Impulse rather than deliberation governs his behaviour among his fellows. To be generous with his money, to help a friend at no matter what risk . . . to hold an unlimited amount of drink, play a good game of solo, tell a good story and wear good clothes.

Few criminals lived up to anywhere near the standards of such an ideal type but it was not an unattractive model to strive towards.

1 THE FRINGES OF THE UNDERWORLD

There was a little pub in Air Street, where Swan and Edgars now stands, where the Bright Young Things of the Gay 'Twenties splashed vintage champagne. A part of the shop that is now Austin Reeds used to be the Chinese restaurant presided over by the prince of London's dope smugglers and white slave traffickers, the infamous Brilliant Chang. There were other clubs in Ham Yard where hardly a night passed without some robbery or violent assault, and the Empire Club underneath the Criterion where a man named Unfreville died suddenly. The first place in Britain where reefer cigarettes – marijuana – were smoked was in the Nest Club in Kingly Street, and there was the Billiards Hall in Wardour Street where you could see wonderful fights any night.

Robert Fabian, *London after Dark* (1954)

Nightlife

The English underworld in the early twentieth century performed a number of illegal but indispensable social services, supplying prostitutes, drugs, gambling and out of hours drinking facilities to the public. In reaction to the horrors of the First World War, the twenties saw an upsurge of hedonism. Despite DORA (The Defence of the Realm Act), which meant that alcohol couldn't be served after 10 p.m., night-clubs mushroomed. Night-clubs varied from expensive and exclusive places that were patronized by the very rich, such as Chez Victor, the Night Light and the Kit Kat Club, to seedy dives which one entered at one's peril. The most interesting were those which seemed to combine the respectability of the former with the excitement and danger of the latter.

While still a teenager Mark Benney graduated from petty larceny to being personal assistant to Con Collins, a typical London wide man, who 'with a magnificent disdain for DORA hired a barn-like hall off Oxford Street, erected a bar at one end and at the other a raised dais for the band' and opened the Falstaff Club. For a brief time the club's air of frenetic excitement induced bolder members of the upper classes to rub shoulders with its mainly underworld clientele, but pitched battles between the 'Raddies' (Italian gangsters, oddly named after the Mazzini/Garibaldi radicals of the nineteenth century) and their racetrack rivals scared them off and made the club an easy target for police clamp-downs.

Kate Meyrick, who became London's 'Night-Club Queen' in the twenties, managed the mixture better. She was the daughter of a well-to-do family in County Clare and something of a rebel – she was the first woman in Ireland to ride a bicycle – but she had married a doctor and disappeared into dull and dreary respectability in Basingstoke. Fabian of the Yard described her as a neat, stern little woman, dressed in blacks and greys, 'who might easily have run a first-class seminary for well-brought-up young ladies'.

By the end of the war she was on her own and had eight children to support. She answered an advertisement for someone to help run 'tea dances'. She was not at all put off when she discovered she would be required to run something less genteel and a few months later she opened Dalton's Club, next door to the Alhambra in Leicester Square. The gangsters who infested the West End provided colour and excitement and, as she ingenuously explained: 'An evening-dress constituted no guarantee at all of its wearer's credentials: a party of apparently quite decent men might easily – only too often did – turn out to be one of the numerous gangs of bullies or racecourse terrorists who held sway.' With their continual demand for free drinks they were a drain on resources but Kate's club did a roaring trade and made a healthy profit. After seven weeks, however, the police raided Dalton's, and at the resulting trial Kate was fined and her club anathematized as 'a hell of iniquity'. Having been 'robbed for ever' of her good name, she threw caution to the winds and opened a succession of clubs – the 43 at 43 Gerrard Street; the Folies Bergère in Newman Street; the Little

Kate Meyrick: happy to be out of Holloway and back among the champagne drinkers.

Club in Golden Square; the Manhattan in Denman Street; and the Silver Slipper in Regent Street, which became the centre of London's nightlife.

Her most famous club, the 43, was patronized by artists and bohemians such as Augustus John, Joseph Conrad, Jacob Epstein and J. B. Priestley when it opened in 1923, but as its fame spread it became the most fashionable night-club in London, attracting a richer clientele as its regulars, and a stream of visiting celebrities – from Russian Bolsheviks and East European aristocrats to American gangsters and film stars. Mrs Meyrick, selling her twelve shilling and sixpence champagne at thirty

shillings during licensing hours and at two pounds afterwards, welcomed them all.

At the 43 Club the underworld and the aristocracy met on equal terms, free-spending burglars like Ruby Sparks mingling with the owners of the jewels and furs from whom they stole. Kate's adopted daughter, Renée Meyrick, recalled nights 'when we would see the cream of Britain's aristocracy sitting at their tables, while practically rubbing shoulders with them would be the roughest and toughest of the underworld, including the Sabini gang, who at that time were up to all sorts of tricks on the racecourses all over England'. Mrs Meyrick complained that underworld characters, particularly the racing gangsters, were too rowdy and dangerous, but the police were much more of a problem.

When fines failed to deter her, more draconian punishment was dealt out. In 1924 she was sentenced to six months in Holloway – not the most salubrious environment for an ailing woman of fifty. Fortunately, her experience of dealing with the diverse, rowdy clientele of her clubs stood her in good stead and she won the affection of the 'hoisters' (shoplifters) who constituted the prison aristocracy. These 'soberly dressed women who looked like churchwardens' wives and swore like troopers' admired her spirit and ensured that she was treated with respect by the other inmates. Outside, her Roedean- and Girton-educated daughters – soon to be married into the aristocracy – continued to run the clubs.

For three years the Meyrick clubs dominated London nightlife. When they were raided and closed they were defiantly re-opened under new names. But on 22 May 1928, the 43 and the Manhattan were raided simultaneously and Kate was given another six-month stretch in Holloway. Worse was to come: while she was serving her sentence rumours reached her of the arrest of Sergeant George Goddard, the officer responsible for leading raids on London clubs. Goddard had received eighty-nine commendations for his work, which had included the first of many raids on the 43 Club, but he had also – on a weekly wage of £6 15s – acquired a luxurious car, a big house and a string of bank accounts and safe-deposit boxes in which were stashed nearly £12,500. Ten days after

coming out of Holloway, Kate was rearrested under the Prevention of Corruption Act and, along with Luigi Ribuffi, the manager of Uncle's Club, charged with bribing a police officer.

Unbeknown to him, Goddard had been under observation for some time, but he was no fool. At the trial he indignantly rejected the prosecution's allegations about his unusual wealth and argued that it was the fruit of legitimate speculation. He told the court that £7,000 came from an unusually lucky streak he had had at the races, £2,000 from foreign exchange dealing, £5,000 from a music publishing venture, while another £4,000 were the profits he made selling 'Wembley Rock' at the British Empire Exhibition of 1924. He was found guilty of 'corruptly receiving money', dismissed from the force for 'flagrant breaches of duty', fined £2,000, and sentenced to eighteen months' hard labour. But the evidence brought forward by the prosecution only accounted for a small portion of Goddard's wealth and he was able to reclaim most of his £12,500. After serving his sentence he retired to a comfortable life of rural respectability.

Mrs Meyrick was less fortunate. She was sentenced to fifteen months' hard labour, which broke her health, if not her spirit. Two further six-month sentences followed before she called it a day and gave an undertaking that she would open no more clubs. Her savings had disappeared when share prices collapsed in the wake of the Wall Street crash and she spent her last year writing her memoirs. She ends with the words: 'What does the future hold in store? It may hold disappointment, perhaps. But one thing I know it never, never can take away from me, and that thing is the love of Life, *real* Life, brilliant and pulsating.' By the time the book was published in 1933, however, the Queen of the Night-Clubs was dead.

Drugs

In Victorian society drug use had been confined to hashish and opium – introspective, contemplative drugs used mainly by middle-class male intellectuals. Drug dealing in cocaine, morphine and heroin flourished during the inter-war years and the twenties drugs scene was centred on emancipated young women determined to 'live for kicks'. A worried writer complained in 1923: 'There is fast springing up in London a horde of female "dopers", women who regularly drug themselves with cocaine and heroin, two of the most potent poisons in the British pharmacopoeia.' He went on to explain that the women who 'doped' themselves were mostly those who led a very doubtful life: 'The only existence they know is bounded by the necessity of preserving their beauty and figure as long as possible.'

The most conspicuous of these 'female dopers', like the actress and adventuress Brenda Dean Paul, were to be found among the Bright Young Things. After the carnage of the 1914–18 war, they saw only hypocrisy and stupidity in the values of their parents and determined to live for pleasure. Their mad whirl of parties and pleasure-seeking shocked but fascinated society. Brenda Dean Paul describes pyjama parties, Greek parties, Russian parties, sailor parties, American parties, murder parties, Mozart parties and bathing parties, where the more daring or more foolish of the older generation tried desperately to keep up with their children. A party at St George's Swimming Baths might have been a brilliant success for those who enjoyed swimming,

but must have been a nightmare for those who couldn't, as the only available seats were the semi-enclosed changing cubicles, dark and stuffy, but by this time the older generation of dowagers had acclimatized themselves to almost anything. Nothing seemed to surprise them any more, and I saw several of them quite contented like plump hens in cubby-holes sitting in dim solitude *en grande tenue*, with lorgnettes fixed at the dripping parade.

The Bright Young Things, with their 'new camaraderie of youth', were not recruited solely from the upper classes and the war, by disposing of a great many brothers, fiancés and husbands, freed rich, young married and unmarried women to pursue their own pleasures. The most famous casualties – Freda Kempton, Billie Carleton, Brenda Dean Paul (who struggled with her addiction into the fifties) – were aspiring actresses and nightclub hostesses rather than whores or society ladies.

The downfall of these and countless other Bright Young Things was blamed on 'Brilliant' Chang, a well-heeled Chinese businessman who owned restaurants in Regent Street and, across the road from the 43, in Gerrard Street. His Oriental inscrutability, his hideaway in the depths of Limehouse (then London's Chinatown) and his involvement

A Bright Young Thing experiments with cocaine.

with fashionable young women made him a fascinating figure to crime writers and their public. His mythological reputation survived into the fifties, when *Daily Mail* crime reporter Arthur Tietjen described him as 'an arch-fiend who stopped at nothing to gain his mastery over beautiful women'. But drugs were probably little more than a sideline for Chang and it was never proved that he was responsible for the deaths of any of the celebrated casualties.

Billie Carleton, a popular young actress of whom great things were expected, died of cocaine poisoning after the victory celebra-tion at the Albert Hall in November 1918. Only the vaguest of rumours connected her to Chang and it was her boyfriend, an adven-turer who went by the name of Reggie de Veuille, who was charged with her man-slaughter. Freda Kempton, a dance hostess at Kate Meyrick's 43 Club, was found dead after an overdose of cocaine in March 1922. Here the link with Chang was more apparent as she had been seen in his company the night before she died. However, as she had made the mistake of falling in love with a married peer (unlike Mrs Meyrick's daugh-ters), her death appears more like a suicide

Brenda Dean Paul: actress and adventuress.

than a case of drug abuse. Brenda Dean Paul, whose bubbling vitality prompted someone to say of her that 'she wakes each morning with a song on her lips', was exposed as a drug addict in the late twenties, but by this time Chang had been deported and her introduction to cocaine and heroin was from a young and very rich Frenchman with whom she enjoyed a loving but platonic relationship until he became jealous and tried to brand her with a white-hot poker.

Ignorance and prejudice about drug use meant that the cure could be more dangerous than the addiction. Brenda Dean Paul was given a dose of hyoscine, which was supposed to put her asleep 'for two or three days'. Instead:

For five hours I writhed without ceasing like a fish in a net, this way and that, sometimes arched back, so that my heels touched the back of my head. I fell on the floor. It took five nurses to hold me down and I remained painfully conscious the whole time in a complete terror of phantasmagoria. The kind of hallucinations and nightmare that no ordinary person could possibly imagine. Terrible faces, quite clear, seeming possessed with some supernatural force, floated before my eyes.

She came out of her 'cure' a tottering, depressive, underweight wreck and her doctor decided she'd be better off taking moderate doses of morphine.

Chang had been arrested in 1924 but the police were only able to pin enough on him

The mysteries of the Orient: 'Brilliant' Chang.

for a fourteen-month sentence, during which time he exasperated the prison censors by writing his letters in Chinese. After serving his sentence he was deported, and though he was sighted in Antwerp and reported 'to be still controlling the London drug traffic through his old accomplices', Chinese involvement in the drug trade was over-exaggerated. A handful of run-down opium dens might have struggled on in Limehouse, but cocaine, morphine and heroin came into the country from Germany rather than China.

In the twenties cocaine production seems to have been virtually unregulated in Germany and the main obstacle for traffickers was smuggling it into Britain. The major figure in the trade was a shadowy Belgian known as Max Blardenburg, whose fabulous wealth enabled him to maintain lavish homes in London, Paris, Berlin and Brussels. He used ex-naval cruisers to run drugs between Belgian and German ports and the east coast of England, making good use of the secluded coves and inlets between Bridlington and Spurn Head. Huge profits could be made from the drug trade as the wholesale price of cocaine was around a pound an ounce and, even before it was broken down into tiny packets that were often adulterated with boric acid, aspirin or powdered milk, the retail price was fifty to sixty-five pounds an ounce. Women seem to have been important as traffickers as well as users, and contemporary crime writers refer in shocked tones to various 'Dope Queens' who were even more unscrupulous than their male counterparts. But the full story of the inter-war 'snowbirds' and 'hopheads' remains shrouded in mystery.

Vice

In Walter Greenwood's novel *Love on the Dole*, the heroine, Sally Hardcastle, gives up on respectable poverty as a mill girl and sells her virtue to the local bookie. *Love on the Dole* captures the hardship and degradation of the Depression of the thirties, but it is unlikely that poverty forced women into prostitution on the same scale it had done in the nineteenth century. Many foreign prostitutes came (or were brought) to Britain and secured themselves against deportation by arranging marriages with impecunious Englishmen.

Women who worked the streets found they could make a surprisingly good living. 'Nutty' Sharpe, head of the Flying Squad in the thirties, estimated that London prostitutes worked four hours a day (or night), during which time they got through fifteen to twenty clients. They charged from ten shillings to a pound a time (sometimes much more) and earned a great deal more than the £2 a week most shop-girls were paid. Marthe Watts, a French prostitute who had worked in the brothels of France, Spain, Italy and North Africa, came to England in 1937 after investing 30,000 francs in an arranged marriage to a drunken Englishman. She found it difficult adjusting to streetwalking. The English weather gave her colds and she was unused to spending so much time on her feet. Englishmen – her clients were predominantly middle class – also had tastes she was not very familiar with and she was 'astonished' at the number of men who wanted her to tie them up and beat them. There were advantages too, though: she was pleasantly surprised at

the reasonableness of the police and the brev-
ity of court proceedings (the American broadcaster and critic Alexander Woollcott was
struck by 'the old world courtesy with which
your magistrates treat your whores') and,
when she adjusted to the English sexual climate and secured a proper 'beat' on Bond
Street, she began to make a lucrative living.

John Worby, a more than usually acute
crook who wrote two volumes of autobiography in the thirties, came across girls who
had given up on dead-end factory jobs and
the drudgery of domestic service to pursue a
more dangerous but more profitable career
as prostitutes. In a break between criminal
activities Worby took a job as a lorry driver
and at a transport café met the road girls,

painted up to the eyes. They were all the same
type, and they drifted, laughing and smoking,
from man to man, making coarse jokes. As I
looked through a window, I saw one being helped
into the back of a lorry. The man followed her in.
She came back into the room about half an hour
later.

On the road to Manchester he picked up a
girl called Flo who told him her story. Like
Jenny, the heroine of Patrick Hamilton's sad,
evocative story *The Siege of Pleasure*, she
was a servant girl who had been enticed,
without much difficulty, from a life of drudgery and petty-minded quibbling to a riskier
but more exciting life of easy virtue. Despite
her hatred of 'the filthy pawing men', she
saw little difference between domestic service
and prostitution: 'In this game I sell a pair of
legs but in the other I sell my whole life.' She
thought there were better prospects for ad-

vancement in her new career, planning, like
many of the girls, to learn the trade on the
road, get together money and a good ward-
robe and move to Piccadilly, 'where we ask a
good price and there are better pickings'.

Other girls were more committed to life on
the road, though they tended to be disdainful
of the attention of lorry drivers and concentrated on commercial travellers. They told
Worby that travellers had more cash and
that they would sometimes go up to Scotland
with one and back again with another. 'The
trip would cost them nothing and they would
stay at the best hotels. It was seldom that
they left these places without some sort of
souvenir, and the traveller was made to pay
pretty high for his comfort.'

Marthe Watts's autobiography, *The Men
in My Life*, lively though it is, tends to fall
into the clichés of repentance which bedevil
so many low-life memoirs. *To Beg I Am
Ashamed*, written by Sheila Cousins in
1938, is startlingly honest and charts the
author's path from filing clerk, shop assistant and door-to-door water-softener sales-
woman to prostitution with little sense of a
descent into the lower depths. She agreed
with 'Nutty' Sharpe that for most prostitutes 'their profession has been a rise in
the world' and gives two examples. First
was

a woman of thirty-odd whom I meet in Piccadilly
often who looks like a little servant-girl. She has a
pug face and wears the plainest taffeta frocks:
before she went on the game she was married to a
fifty shillings a week railwayman and had five
children. Now, she told me, she kept a five pound
a week flat and a maid.'

THE FRINGES OF THE UNDERWORLD 15

Then there was 'a tall, ungainly girl, nearly six feet high, who plods down the pavement with a scrap of mangy fur round her collar', who kept two places, 'one for lumber and one to live in', and gave her ponce twenty pounds a week. Sheila Cousins thought the twenties good for business but complained of the war wrecks: 'limping, drunken ex-officers, with a leery fatherliness that turned sour when the door shut'. Thirties customers were apparently more amenable, but there was unfair competition from the imported French-women, whom she describes uncomplimentarily as 'hard-bitten professionals, shapeless as sacks and over forty, who spoil the market by taking even ten shillings from a man'.

The control of prostitution rackets tended to be the preserve of foreigners and outsiders, and was much despised by the rest of the criminal fraternity. Eddie Manning, a Jamaican dope dealer who operated from a basement club in Berwick Street, maintained a tenuous control over a string of girls in the twenties. As a young constable, Fabian of the Yard was told he was 'the worst man in London', but this seems to have stemmed more from the horror and disgust with which 'respectable' society viewed a black man having sexual power over white women than from any outrageously heinous activities he indulged in. He was arrested in 1924 and when he re-emerged after three years' penal servitude he found it difficult to re-establish himself. The cellar club he opened in Berwick Street was constantly raided and in 1929 he was given another lagging. Val Davis, whose *Gentlemen of the Broad Arrows* is an acute if sometimes sentimental account of his own

ten years' penal servitude, met him in Parkhurst in 1933. He discovered that Manning's real name was Freddie Simpson and he'd come to England during the war and worked in a munitions factory before becoming a jazz drummer and drifting into pimping and drug-dealing. 'He had aged a great deal since I last saw him, his black crispy locks were plentifully streaked with grey and his dark skin could not conceal an unhealthy pallor beneath.' He was suffering acutely from cocaine withdrawal and well-intentioned gifts of chewing-tobacco only made him sick. Within three months he was dead.

For most of the twenties the dominant vice gangs were European. Until 1929 the leading figures were a Frenchman, Casimir Micheletti, and a Spanish dancer, Juan Antonio Castanar (the man responsible for introducing the tango into England), whose dancing school in Archer Street served as a useful recruiting agency for the white slave trade. There seems to have been no love lost between the two men and on Easter Monday 1926 another French pimp, Charles 'Bateleur' (Charles the Acrobat), was found in a pool of blood in the Cochon Club in Frith Street. 'Bateleur' was a friend of Micheletti and when the murderer, 'Mad Emile' Berthier, was caught on the Newhaven ferry he half admitted that he had killed 'Bateleur' in mistake for Micheletti, though he denied that he was working for Castenar. In 1929 the police, unable to muster enough evidence to convict the two pimps, had them both deported, Micheletti to France, Castanar to Spain. By 1930 they had both drifted to Paris and were trying to ply their old trade in Montmartre. A violent argument between them led to Micheletti being shot through the heart and Castanar being imprisoned for life on Devil's Island.

Back in England, Emil Allard, a Latvian also known as Max Kessel or Red Max, took over and survived until 1936, when the discovery of a bullet-ridden corpse with manicured hands, a scarred face and patent leather shoes in a ditch outside St Albans suggested that another upheaval had occurred in the deeper reaches of the underworld. Red Max's murderer turned out to be another Frenchman, Marcel Vernon (known in England as George Edward Lacroix), who had escaped from Devil's Island and ran a white slave trade ring with bases in Ven-

ezuela, Haiti, the United States, Canada and Soho. He was deported to France, found guilty of Max's murder and returned to Devil's Island. At his trial sensational details were revealed of how adventurous young women were lured to exotic locations with promises of jobs as mannequins and secretaries, dancers and cabaret artists, and forced into prostitution.

The white slave trade was a subject which much occupied the public imagination between the wars. One expert, Henri Champly, explains in *The Road to Shanghai* that, as a result of fashion, travel and the cinema,

the South Sea Islanders, the Africans, the American negroes, in fact the Coloured people all over the world have become convinced that the

Marcel Vernon and Suzanne Bertron on trial for the murder of Red Max the Latvian.

white woman is the most beautiful, the most voluptuous – in short, that she is superior to all others. They prefer her, they desire her – and they beckon to her.

The Road to Shanghai was a best-seller, as was its predecessor, *The Road to Buenos Ayres* by Albert Londres, though neither book confirmed suspicions that innocent young European women were being dragged off into sexual bondage in far-off lands. Both Champly and Londres came to the conclusion that the great majority of women who made the journey to South America or China did so willingly, with the intention of either marrying a rich client or saving enough money to retire on. The novelist Theodore Dreiser, in his introduction to Londres's *The Road to Buenos Ayres*, stresses that for many women who travelled along it, it was by no means the road to ruin: 'In the end, instead of dying early and in the gutter or madhouse or gaol, as the worthy religionist of our day would have us believe, the erring do no more than retire to other and not infrequently more profitable and much more respectable lines of effort.' Returning to France they became owners of bars – or brothels, shops and lodging houses – and forgot about their shady past. But not all prostitutes fared so well.

When as far from home as Buenos Aires or Shanghai, it was not easy for a woman discontented with her lot to return. Those who had been shipped out with the connivance of their desperately poor families, such as the large contingent of Polish Jewesses in the Argentine, were often too timid and inexperienced to do much about their miserable lot. And Londres's pimps, though they come

Eddie Manning – the wickedest man in London? This policeman obviously thinks so.

across as witty and charming, were vicious and unscrupulous in maintaining control over their women. One of them confided to him: 'Our women are penny-in-the-slot machines. We mustn't break the machines, we must be satisfied to shake them up a bit from time to time.'

Not all women who went abroad did so as prostitutes. The female adventuress, fascinatingly glimpsed in Alfred Hitchcock's film *Rich and Strange* (1931), was a feature of the inter-war years and she generally knew how to manipulate the prestige owing to white women. Brenda Dean Paul, for example, tiring of London, Paris and drugs, and wanting to see the world, seems to have successfully kept her close relationships with men at a platonic level and felt no danger whatsoever of being kidnapped into white slavery.

2 THE POLICEMAN'S LOT

The talks on discipline were impressive – and frightening. We learned not to talk to each other on duty – the crime of 'gossiping'; not to talk to young women, particularly nursemaids: not to be found absent off the beat; not to smoke or drink on duty. We were warned that we would be severely punished if caught. We had some practice with the truncheon, a fifteen-inch length of hard wood known as 'Mr Wood', and were told never to aim at a person's head but to go for his shoulders or arms. We were also told to keep a tight hold on it, for many a policeman has been hit with his own truncheon.

Peter Beveridge, *Inside the C.I.D.* (1957)

The bobby on the beat

The reputation of the police in the inter-war years was better than it had been in Victorian times but bobbies were still regarded with slightly contemptuous condescension by the middle classes and outright hostility by the poor. Not surprisingly, the underpaid uniformed policemen, most of whom spent the whole of their career as constables, were susceptible to bribery, and made free use of Johnny Wood (the truncheon) when not receiving a share in the profits of crime. A verse from a popular song indicates the widespread belief that British bobbies stole from those too drunk and incapable to resist:

> Every member of the force
> Has a watch and chain of course
> If you want to know the time
> Ask a policeman

The police were poorly housed and poorly paid until the fifties, when full employment and the post-war crime boom forced an improvement. In 1938 a constable's pay was sixty-two shillings a week with six shillings rent allowance and one shilling boot allowance. Good digs cost around thirty shillings and the uninviting alternative was the police section house. Peter Beveridge, who joined the Metropolitan Police as a constable in 1919, was sent to the section house in Whitechapel. His description of life there makes it sound little more comfortable than a Salvation Army hostel:

On each floor were a number of cubicles with wooden walls that stopped about two feet from the ceiling. There was an iron bedstead, a hard chair and a steel locker with only a few shelves for clothes. At intervals down the corridor spluttered gas lamps so that only certain cubicles were reasonably well lighted. Mine was certainly not one of those, for there was a simple rule of the section house which allowed the old hands to take the best cubicles, or bunks, as they were called.

John Capstick found similar conditions at the Adelphi Street Police Institute in the twenties. It had just one large dormitory for the dozen or so policemen billeted there; they slept on straw mattresses and 'snored like foghorns'.

Beveridge and Capstick, like most bright and ambitious policemen, moved from the uniformed branch into the CID at the first opportunity. Robert Mark, who became Commissioner of the Metropolitan Police in the early seventies, was unusual in rising through the hierarchy with no experience of detective work. He joined the Manchester force in the late thirties and found that, in contrast to his own middle-class grammar-school background, most of his fellow recruits were working-class ex-servicemen, and that the police ethos left a great deal to be desired.

The Manchester force was dominated by a philosophy not unlike that of Victoria's army. There was no suggestion of leadership by example. Seniors battened on and bullied juniors and the force did the same to that part of the public not able to look after itself. There was a kind of comradeship born of sharing the same conditions and there were plenty of basically kind and decent men. But the system was harsh, unimaginative, unintelligent and ruthless.

Mark soon gave up worrying about the futility of shaking hands with doorknobs all night and like most of his colleagues 'rapidly acquired a knowledge of unlocked outside lavatories in which I could smoke a peaceful pipe out of the wind'.

Improvements in police efficiency didn't necessarily make the policeman's lot a happier one. The invention of the police box – a wooden hut with an electric fire, a telephone and a blue lamp which could be switched on from divisional headquarters to attract attention – in the late twenties extended police control over city life but it made the job of the bobby on the beat depressingly lonely. As Robert Mark complained: 'No consideration at all was given to physical comfort, the value of contact with fellow officers or the need to promote a sense of corporate identity.' The constable 'reported for duty' by ringing in from the box fifteen minutes before relieving his colleague on the previous shift and 'signed off' in the same way. Meal-times were spent in the box and, though there were no cooking facilities, each box was provided with a list of nearby places where people were friendly enough to offer hot water for brewing tea. Signing on and off by telephone closed the gap in police patrols – fully exploited by criminals – when constables were too busy making their way to or from the police station to worry about crime. But for Mark at least, 'It was a weird life. The only policemen you saw were those on adjoining beats, the section sergeant twice nightly and the patrol inspector.'

Crushing the city gangs

The police box was one of the innovations introduced by Sir Percy Sillitoe when he took over as Chief Constable of Sheffield in 1926. Sillitoe was an unconventional and charismatic figure within the dull ranks of the uniformed police. At nineteen he had signed on as a trooper in the British South African Police and risen to become a captain by the end of the First World War. In 1923 he returned to England to become Chief Constable of Chesterfield, moving to the East Riding in 1925 and taking up his appointment in Sheffield a year later at the age of thirty-eight. He was to become known in the popular press as 'Britain's Ace Gang Buster' and in the late forties became the only uniformed policeman ever to become head of MI5. Police boxes were seen as an important organizational advance and were soon adopted by the Metropolitan Police in London, but Sillitoe is best known for his vigorous campaigns against the Sheffield and Glasgow gangs.

The rival gangs of Sam Garvin and George Mooney terrorized Sheffield in the twenties and appeared to rule the poorer areas of the city with impunity. According to the *Sheffield Mail*, the gangsters were something more than ignorant ruffians. 'They are men who have calculated quite coolly and calmly the gains to be won by their terrifying outlawry. They are prepared to put up a stiff fight for supremacy.' And indeed they did. The fact that they rarely used guns hardly made their violence less effective. They drew protection money from shopkeepers, publicans and bookmakers but their real power lay in the 'tossing rings' they organized at Skye Edge, Wadsley, Five Arches and Tinsley on the rural outskirts of Sheffield.

To prevent the police disrupting their

highly elaborate games of pitch and toss, the gangsters employed 'crows' and 'pikers' to warn of possible raids and secured the services of respected 'ponters' to adjudicate between those participating in the game. Costs were covered by a toll (half a crown in the pound) levied on all bets made and this generally left the gang leaders with a substantial profit. Sillitoe claimed: 'Each gang had hundreds of members, and they were almost unchecked in their villainies. They had no hesitation about swarming around a police officer and attacking him if he tried to interfere with their betting or other criminal activities.' Rivalry between the two gangs over the control of these lucrative enterprises led to vicious beatings and at least one murder, which gave Sillitoe the excuse he needed to crush them.

Sillitoe's predecessor, Lieutenant-Colonel Hall-Dalwood, had already formed a 'Flying Squad' of four very big, very tough constables with the remit to enter pubs and eject trouble-making gang members. Sillitoe expanded the squad and brought in the European Ju-Jitsu Champion, Harry Hunter, to train them. The gangsters were now confronted by a force of well-trained men ready, willing and able to meet force with force, brutality with brutality, by beating up anyone foolish enough to challenge their authority. Within a year the power of the gangs was broken.

Sillitoe became Chief Constable of Glasgow in 1931 and used similar tactics against the 'Parlour Boys', the 'Billy Boys' and the 'Norman Conks'. As in Sheffield, the gangs terrorized parts of the city. Apparently the usual technique employed with shopkeepers who chose not to contribute was to mix all the shop goods in a smashed heap on the floor, with the proprietor on top of the pile 'like a bruised Guy Fawkes'. Protection money (along with petty burglary) was necessary to secure an income for gang members, but at least as much energy was spent in fighting rival gangs. Crafty as well as brutal, Glasgow gangsters got their 'queens' to carry hatchets, swords and sharpened bicycle chains to the scenes of their battles. As Sillitoe explained: 'This was because they knew that the police dare not interfere with or search a girl, who would at once protest that the officers were improperly assaulting her.' However, the police had few inhibitions about maltreating suspected gangsters who fell into their hands, and 'Sillitoe's Cossacks', as his strong-arm men were called, acquired a still-remembered reputation for brutality. In effect Sillitoe was demonstrating that the police could operate as a tougher and more efficient gang with infinitely greater resources. The old rough-house types who had openly challenged the power of the police were graudually tamed, but their places were taken by more sophisticated criminals who were prepared to work with the police; and the profits to be taken from the illegal gambling industry made bribery and corruption worthwhile for both sides.

Scotland Yard

Unlike most European countries, Britain has never had a national police force. Until 1931 there were 182 separate local forces and

Scotland Yard by night.

even after amalgamations were carried out in the interests of economy and efficiency there were still 126, ranging in size from 100 to 2,800 men. By far the biggest of these forces – employing almost a third of the total number of police – was the Greater London Metropolitan Police force controlled from Scotland Yard. The size of the Met meant that it tended to dominate police affairs and smaller forces would generally be expected to call in Scotland Yard's detectives to deal with their most serious crimes. However, the Commissioner of the Metropolitan Police had no formal control over the Chief Constables of even the smallest provincial force. As Sir Harold Scott, (who ran Scotland Yard in the late forties) tactfully explained, the rela-

tionship of the Met to smaller forces 'is in no way that of a controller, but rather that of a friendly older brother in a large family'.

Traditional images of Scotland Yard give the impression that it is solely concerned with detective work, but in the thirties a mere 1,400 of the Met's 20,000 men were detectives, and of them only around 400 were based at Scotland Yard. The remainder were distributed round the twenty-four divisions into which the Greater London area was divided. Large numbers of those employed at Scotland Yard worked in mundane backwaters like the Criminal Records Office and the Fingerprint Department, or at co-ordinating the activities of the river police and the traffic police. Public attention focused on the more glamorous activities of those small élites employed in the Special Branch and the Flying Squad.

Flying Squad driver 'Jack' Frost commented, 'There is nothing, externally, very notable about Britain's anti-crime generals – they are all quiet, clean-shaven, and unassuming.' Nevertheless it was the solid, phlegmatic, intrepid quality of the Scotland Yard detective which captured the public imagination, and from the twenties to the late fifties Scotland Yard's 'big five' – top detectives leading the Flying Squad or given charge of well-publicized murder cases – were constantly in the news. This image was fostered by the depiction of Scotland Yard detectives in films, from John Longden in Hitchcock's *Blackmail* in 1929 to Jack Hawkins in John Ford's *Gideon of the Yard* nearly thirty years later. Such screen detectives tended to be hard-working, orderly, respectable and marked by a certain flinty integrity.

No doubt these qualities were shared by their real-life counterparts but they tended to be mixed with more venal ones. Mary Grigg, writing about the famous corruption case of 'Mad Harry' Challenor in the early sixties, points out that:

The public expects the police force to combat crime; and it also expects the police to do this successfully without the slightest impropriety. Police officers had discovered in practice, however, that they could either catch criminals or behave properly, but that it was difficult to do both. They were therefore dithering constantly between satisfying the public in one respect and not offending it in the other.

Challenor, who would plant incriminating evidence on suspects with a friendly, 'Here you are, a present from Uncle Harry', had

Twenties technology: inside a Flying Squad tender.

got beyond caring about the public. But the dilemma outlined by Mary Grigg tended to divide detectives into two camps: the 'chair-polishers', who did everything by the book, and those more interesting if more dubious characters prepared to mingle in the underworld, befriend criminals and build up a network of informers. Their predecessors go back at least as far as the eighteenth-century thief-taker and master criminal Jonathan Wild.

Charles Raven, a successful thief turned writer, reckoned that around 90 per cent of convictions for serious crime came from informers, and the memoirs of successful Scotland Yard detectives like Peter Beveridge, John Gosling and Robert Fabian stress that the detective is only as good as his network of informers. This was particularly so in the Flying Squad, which dealt exclusively with professional criminals – safe-breaking gangs, receivers, protection racketeers, and 'jump-up merchants' specializing in the theft of loaded lorries. Here, inside information was essential. 'Nutty' Sharpe, a leading thirties detective, thought that the more crooks a Flying Squad man could get to know, the more valuable would be his contribution to crime detection. And Inspector Bob Higgins, writing in the fifties, stated firmly, 'Policemen and detectives without extensive experience of the criminal's habits are of no use for Squad work.' An aura of venality surrounds both Sharpe and Higgins, but both of them managed to keep the respect of their superiors and that of the underworld.

Informers (generally known as 'snouts' by the police and 'grasses' by the crooks) be-trayed their fellows for a variety of reasons: out of spite or a need for revenge (ponces only tended to be arrested when the prostitutes they lived off 'shopped' them); out of fear (particularly ageing criminals unwilling to face another long prison sentence); or for the money. The Police Informants Fund seldom paid out more than £15 and generally dealt in shillings rather than pounds, but the insurance companies offered large rewards for the recovery of stolen valuables. According to Robert Fabian:

A small job may pay only a few shillings. But a big robbery can be worth hundreds of pounds to the nark, from insurance rewards which the police collect for them. The nark gets 10 per cent of the insured value, which is often more than the stuff is worth to the thief.

A grass's life was not often a long and happy one. Much of the work of the chiv-men involved striking terror into the hearts of informers and potential informers, and once 'the mark of the nark' – a long, jagged razor cut ending at the edge of the mouth – had been left on a victim he would be shunned by underworld society.

Such dire penalties were an indication of the difficulty of keeping anything secret in the underworld. John Gosling, a maverick detective whose career with the 'Ghost Squad' failed to win him the promotion he expected, became something of an expert on informing, collaborating on the script of Ken Annakin's film *Death of a Snout* (released in 1963 as *The Informers*). He explained:

Like the respectable professions, the criminal world is a small one in which 'shop' is talked constantly. Almost everyone knows everyone else, either in person or by repute. A good job is discussed by those who did not do it as lawyers will discuss a QC's brilliant defence line, or a journalist a good scoop. They will discuss these things even with a policeman, when the policeman has won their confidence.

Thus some grasses enjoyed long and successful careers exploiting the garrulousness of their fellow criminals. John Gosling's Tommy the Talker, who had 'a rooted aversion to hard work, and after a few months "inside" an equally deep hatred of prison', and Robert Fabian's 'Hymie the Gambler' ('Big Hubby' Distelman), who first surfaced in the mid-thirties and was still around twenty years later, became so adept at their double game that they avoided the horrible reprisals meted out to the Judases of the underworld.

It was difficult for a police detective not to be drawn into semi-criminal activities and the possibility of corruption was (and is) a constant danger. An informer could be expected to be absolved of his own criminal activities provided he continued to betray his colleagues, and this could lead to a virtual licensing of certain criminals to operate. If activity was slack it was a simple matter for the informer to act as *agent provocateur* and set something up. The rewards of such artificially induced crime didn't necessarily end with the imprisonment of the dupes who had carried out the robbery. If everything went successfully the snout would collect insurance money and be encouraged to share it with his police partner. John Gosling, writing in the late fifties when worries about police corruption had put the chair-polishers in control, commented sadly that:

In the dangerous world of crime it is easy for a policeman to put a foot wrong and if he does so it means curtains to his career. The link my colleagues and I built up with the underworld have been weakened ... Yet, despite all the scientific advances achieved in the realms of thief-taking, the use of the informer in the detection of crime remains as vital as ever. I hope with all my heart that the policy of non-encouragement does not lead to its extinction.

Accusations of police corruption in the sixties, seventies, eighties and nineties show that Gosling's fears of extinction were premature.

3 THE RACETRACK GANGS

The surprise at first was far worse than the pain (a nettle could sting as badly). 'You fools,' he said, 'it's not me, it's him you want,' and turned and saw the faces ringing him all round. They grinned back at him: every man had his razor out: and he remembered for the first time Colleoni laughing up the telephone wire. The crowd had scattered at the first sight of trouble; he heard Spicer call out, 'Pinkie. For Christ's sake'; an obscure struggle reached its climax out of his sight. He had other things to watch: the long cut-throat razors which the sun caught slanting low down over the downs from Shoreham. He put his hand to his pocket to get his blade, and the man immediately facing him leant across and slashed his knuckles . . . One of them leant forward to cut his cheek, and when he put up his hand to shield himself they slashed his knuckles again. He began to weep, as the four-thirty went by in a drum-beat of hooves beyond the rail.

Graham Greene, *Brighton Rock* (1938)

The respectable working classes? A racetrack crowd.

Betting on horses

In the early nineteenth century prize fighting and horse racing provided ample opportunities for theft, trickery and violence. The brutality and rowdiness of prize fight matches became increasingly unacceptable as Victorian society embraced sobriety and respectability and the sport lost its aristocratic patronage. But at racetracks the wealthiest and the most disreputable elements of society continued to mingle. From the middle of the nineteenth century onwards efforts were made to clean up the unsavoury image of horse racing by enclosing courses and eradicating the fairground nature of race meetings. The notoriously rough suburban London tracks at Streatham, Bromley, Enfield, Harrow, Kingsbury, West Drayton and Croydon were closed down and replaced by fully enclosed and well-policed park courses at Sandown, Kempton, Lingfield and Hurst Park. Here, as in Association Football grounds and *Palais de Danses*, the respectable working class paid a fee to enjoy a commercially organized leisure activity and undesirables could be turned back at the turnstiles. However, disreputable elements remained and fraudsters, tricksters and beggars still reigned over the free side of the older courses like Epsom and Ascot.

One had to be rich to own racehorses, but

not to bet on them. The working classes soon picked up the habit of betting on horse races and before long bookmakers realized that a high volume of small bets from the working-class punter could be safer and more lucrative than the infrequent big aristocratic wager. In the 1890s several new racecourses were opened and cheap excursion trains ferried in crowds of relatively prosperous working-class racegoers. But by this time the racecourse was not the only place where one could make a bet.

Once the electric telegraph system was completed in the 1840s, the press was able to publish results and starting price odds quickly enough for off-course betting to become viable. 'List shops' proliferated, so called because of the lists of runners posted up for the convenience of those who wished to bet. A celebrated racing correspondent, 'The Druid', calculated that by the early 1850s there were around four hundred in London alone. Middle-class alarm at this manifestation of working-class gambling led to them being outlawed in 1853 and bookmakers running betting houses, exhibiting lists or soliciting bets became liable to a £100 fine and six months' imprisonment.

The closure of the list shops merely pushed the bookies, who relied on the sixpences and shillings of the working man, out on to the streets. This prompted further protest and further legislation. After the 1906 Street Betting Act was passed, any person loitering for the purposes of taking or making bets could be fined £10 for a first offence, £20 for a second, and £50 or six months' imprisonment for a third. Not until the Betting and Gaming Act 1960 was passed was the working man legally permitted to place bets off the racecourse. Nevertheless, Betting Duty returns of the twenties show that there were some 14,625 bookmakers in existence and no doubt some evaded the count altogether. Ways were devised of avoiding the penalties and street betting became a ubiquitous part of working-class life in the first half of the twentieth century. Bookies' scouts and runners prowled the streets, attracting a continual flow of furtive transactions. Off the streets, in pubs, barbers, newsagents, small general stores, someone could generally be found to take a bet and bookies staked out regular pitches outside factory gates and employment exchanges. Big industrial enterprises – shipyards, steelworks, mills and factories – had secret networks of touts and sub-touts. The Select Committee on Betting Duty complained in 1932:

Work in our mills and factories is stopped and damaged by the amount of time given to the discussion and thought about betting ... A class of persons of many thousands has grown up which lives entirely by giving tips and information ... The streets of our towns are perambulated by bookmakers or their betting agents inviting persons to bet with them.

And Ross McKibbin explains how, paradoxically, 'The immediate result of making cash betting illegal was to make it public.' The scouts and runners of the street bookmakers seemed to be everywhere, their presence adding an air of furtive excitement to town life. 'Such activity, necessarily hurried and agitated, made it seem as if betting was becoming the principal business of the country.'

Had the police tried to enforce the Street Betting Act rigorously they could have provoked a situation analagous to that in America in the twenties when Prohibition and the profits from the illicit liquor trade gave an enormous boost to gangland violence. In Britain the police took the pragmatic view that the law was impossible to enforce. Sir Trevor Bigham, the Assistant Commissioner of the Metropolitan Police, told the Royal Commission on Lotteries and Betting in 1932:

These particular laws have a bad influence on police administration. They put the police, who should be the friends of the law-abiding public, in a position of antagonism to a very large part of it . . . Moreover, both the police and the public know that, even if strictly enforced, these laws would operate mainly against the humbler class of gambler, and this does not foster a feeling of respect for them.

What made the system particularly unfair was that it was perfectly legal for people with big bank balances, who could afford to have a credit account with a bookmaker, to bet off-course on credit by letter, telegraph or telephone.

To satisfy the letter of the law while disavowing its substance, an elaborate charade was played out whereby the bookies made available to the courts a regular supply of bodies who would plead guilty and be fined. The bookies then financially recompensed them for their troubles. According to Arthur Harding, an East End hard-man occasionally employed by bookmakers to protect them:

In every division the police had two men whose job it was to take the bookmakers in. They didn't have to hide in a cart or anything like that, they'd come round quite polite and say, 'Albert, stick a man up tomorrow, we're having a raid.' Well all we had to do was find a man who was hard up – any Tom, Dick or Harry – and say, 'Here's a chance to earn yourself a couple of quid', and they'd say, 'Oh blimey, yes.' They'd stand in the street, and then the plain-clothes man would take them in and charge them with illegal betting . . . It was all part of the game.

The police, too, received their fees for participating in a game that seemed to satisfy everybody. In Whitechapel in the twenties the bookmaker Jimmy Smith, a respected figure despite being partly paralysed after falling into a fire when drunk, 'used to settle up with the police in Commercial Street Station. A police constable got a shilling a day, sergeants and inspectors got more and at Christmas time they all got a bonus, sometimes a crate of whisky.' The courts were well aware of what was going on and would rarely waste more than a couple of minutes on a case. Sometimes such peremptory treatment brought about a comically embarrassing situation – as when one bookie's runner hopped out of the dock on a wooden leg.

Illegal gambling became a huge industry in Britain in the inter-war years and it was hardly surprisingly that such a profitable industry should invite the attention of protection gangs. (Estimates put its annual turnover at somewhere between £350 million and £450 million, a figure larger than that of any other industry except the building trade.) Between 1918 and 1956 the underworld was dominated by the race gang bosses – Darby Sabini, Alf White and Jack Spot.

The incorrigible Darby Sabini (right).

The rise of Darby Sabini

At racecourses large sums of money changed hands in relatively isolated surroundings, making the bookies, even more than winning punters, vulnerable to robbery and violence. Moreover, because control over the right to erect a stand and operate as a bookmaker at a racecourse was often ill-defined it was open to exploitation. Accordingly, the race gangs offered protection to bookies and allocated the best pitches to those they favoured most. Until the early twenties the racing scene was dominated by Billy Kimber and his Birmingham gang (known as the Brummagem Boys), though Kimber drew recruits from Hoxton and the Elephant and Castle as well as Birmingham. Their activities provoked the Jockey Club into setting up special squads of racecourse police. More sophisticated gangsters realized that new methods were necessary if the racecourses were to continue to provide a lucrative source of income.

Darby Sabini and his brothers Joe, Charles, Harry Boy and Fred came from Saffron Hill, the heart of the Italian community in Clerkenwell, and in the early twenties they wrested control of the lucrative south of England racecourses from Kimber and his Brummagem Boys. Arthur Harding explains:

The Birmingham mob were all English chaps, all 'rough house'. They weren't as clever as the Darby Sabini lot. Darby Sabini got in with the Flying Squad, they got in with the racecourse police, so they had the police on their side, protecting them. Directly there was any fighting, it was always the Birmingham mob who got pinched. They was always getting time, five-year sentences and that. In the end Billy Kimber decided they'd have to go back to Birmingham.

Actually the contrast between old and new was not quite so straightforward. The sartorially elegant Harry Boy Sabini looked like one might expect an Anglo-Italian gangster to look, with his thin moustache and sharp suits, but Darby, the boss, barrel-chested, cloth-capped and with collarless shirt and flashy choker, looked more a traditional English tough than a *mafioso*. And Billy Kimber, far from being a punch-drunk provincial thug, was intelligent and resourceful. When a gang of welching bookies aroused the fury of racegoers at the 1919 St Leger meeting at Doncaster, it was Kimber's calming influence which prevented a riot. He was not without his allies among the racecourse police. Ex-Chief Inspector Tom Divall, who had risen from the ranks to become one of the top four Scotland Yard detectives before seeking the fresh air and fun of the racecourses, regarded him as 'one of the best' and praised his 'soothing and tactful way of speaking'. And well he might, Kimber having saved him from being badly beaten up more than once.

The Sabinis claimed to be freeing bookmakers from the oppression and extortion of the 'Brummagem Hammers', and if bookmakers were too fly to put much faith in Sabini's Bookmakers and Backers Racecourse Protection Society, there was more logic in a London gang controlling the south of England courses than a Birmingham one. The bookmakers themselves were ambivalent about the racing gangsters. As T. H. Dey wrote in his *Leaves from a Bookmaker's Book* in 1930: 'I have often been of service to the "boys" – it pays a professional racegoer to be, and politeness costs nothing. I have never refused to subscribe a "quid" or so to every subscription list that has been placed before me by "responsible" people.' The bookmaker who decided not to pay 'chalk money', or 'pitch or stand money', or that he had no use for 'dots and dashes' and 'twist cards', was liable to have his stand wrecked, his satchel turned upside down and its valuable contents scattered, his book torn to shreds and his physical well-being severely threatened. Nevertheless, the divide between honest bookie and race gang villain was often a thin one.

Violent friends could be useful in lots of ways to a bookie. Gambling debts were not enforceable by law and in the early twenties Ladbrokes, the largest and most respectable of bookmaking firms, estimated that $12\frac{1}{2}$ per cent of the money owed to them at that time was unlikely to be recovered. Less reputable bookies were unwilling to give up so gracefully and a couple of the 'boys' would be sent round to potential defaulters to remind them of their obligations. It was also to the bookie's advantage if his clerk and tic-tac man could also double up as his bodyguards. And it was the ambition of every clerk and tic-tac man, whether or not he was a member of a gang, to erect a stand and become a bookie in his own right. As T. H. Dey explained:

Many of the 'boys', once they get a 'touch', turn over a new leaf, become respectable, taking on a job as 'tic-tac', bookmaker, professional backer, or getting into some commercial business. Many such I know, who are now heads of flourishing businesses, were at one time cold-blooded 'welshers', 'three-card' tricksters, 'confidence' men and 'crooks' generally – but who am I – or any of us for that matter – to criticize or expose them?

The Sabinis worked in close co-operation with a group of up-and-coming Jewish bookmakers – Edward Emmanuel, Snoutie Parker, Shimmer Josephs, Moey Levy and Deafy Schwartz – who needed Sabini's help to establish themselves on the racecourses. Edward

Emmanuel was responsible for the production of printed lists of runners and the intricately coloured tickets given by bookies to their clients as acknowledgements of their bets, and through the influence of the Sabinis they were sold at substantial profits to other bookmakers. Darby Sabini himself, despite his unsmooth appearance, seems to have had considerable diplomatic talents, and is remembered with affection in respectable as well as unrespectable quarters. With the help of his four brothers he was able to maintain a more cohesive and orderly mob than the Brummagem Boys. (Though according to one source at least, it was his sister who became the organizing force behind the racketeering, having taken over the running of the family after their mother's death.) In most of the encounters between the two sides it was the Birmingham gang which came off worst, though their most disastrous escapade had nothing to do with any connivance between the police and the Sabinis. In a large-scale attack on the road to Epsom just before the 1921 Derby the Birmingham mob hijacked a charabanc full of bookies and toughs and proceeded to lay into them with coshes, choppers, bricks, bludgeons and iron bars:

Men were knocked out and were trampled on as they fell in the roadway. The most deliberate savagery was practised. Residents of roadside cottages screamed. The shouts attracted more attention. Traffic was held up for a few moments until the attacked scattered. Then the Birminghmam gang got back in their charabanc and cleared off.

It was not until they were celebrating their victory that the truth emerged: far from defeating the Sabinis they had attacked a party of Leeds bookmakers and their protectors who had hitherto been allies of the Birmingham gang.

Several times between 1921 and 1924 the Brummagem Boys did manage to find the Sabinis and give battle, though it was rare for members of the public to be involved in these affrays. The jockey Tommy Weston, whose contacts with the underworld eventually brought him into trouble with the Jockey Club, recalled that at the 1924 Derby meeting he bumped into a Midlands acquaintance who,

dipping into his hip pocket, pulled out a revolver saying: 'There are three hundred of us here, all armed. If you hear guns cracking, take no notice. Keep going. All our lads from Birmingham are here to shoot up the London boys who have been up to some of their tricks with us again.'

The threat failed to materialize though, and the Birmingham mob gradually retreated north and acknowledged their subordinate position. Kimber himself was shot and left for dead after an abortive truce meeting at the home of bookmaker Walter Beresford, but he seems to have made a full recovery and is last heard of in 1930 on the managerial staff of the Wimbledon Greyhound stadium.

The most dangerous attack on Darby Sabini was on his home ground, the Fratalanza Club in Great Bath Street. One quiet evening in November 1922, a rival Italian family, the four Cortesi brothers, arrived unannounced and began shooting at the Sabinis. Fortunately their expertise with firearms left something to be desired: Darby escaped unscathed, Harry Boy Sabini caught a bullet in the stomach trying to shield Louisa Dorali, the club-owner's daughter, and the would-be assassins were quickly rounded up. Great Bath Street was only a short walk from Fleet Street and the shooting aroused a flurry of press interest. The *Daily Express* did its best to heighten the drama by putting out a colourful description of the most prominent of the gunmen:

[He was] sharp featured, five foot eight inches tall, with sallow complexion, brown hair, grey eyes and a pronounced Roman nose . . . [He] walks with a Charlie Chaplin step, the result of flat feet and knock knees, but he is said to be able to disguise not only his walk but his features. Detectives believe that he took refuge in a house not a hundred yards from the Fratalanza Club and emerged in the disguise of an old woman.

This master of disguise turned out to be the excitable but singularly unferocious Enrico Cortesi, a hatmaker of hitherto unblemished character who, like his brothers, obediently gave himself up to the police as soon as he heard he was wanted.

Enrico protested that he knew of a dozen cases where men had been stabbed or shot by the Sabinis and no legal action had been taken. Darby Sabini responded by claiming that he was a very quiet and peaceable man, and turned out his pockets in court just to show that he had no revolver. The feuding aspect of the case fascinated Mr Justice Darling, who in his summing up told the jury that the case reminded him of the old Italian feud between the Montagues and Capulets. He commented sagely that: 'Although these parties could combine against people whom they held to be a common enemy, they were always quarrelling among themselves.' These august historical precedents seemed to have worked in favour of the Cortesis. Only Enrico and one of his brothers were found guilty, and for the offence of 'shooting with intent to murder' they escaped with the lenient sentence of three years' penal servitude.

Jews and Italians

In the twenties relations between the Jewish community in Whitechapel and the Italians in Clerkenwell were amicable and the Sabini gang recruited Jewish heavies and protected Jewish bookmakers. But Fascist-sponsored trips to the homeland re-awakened old prejudices and Darby Sabini found his gang riven with internal dissension as anti-semitism spread in the Italian community. Weakened by these divisions, the Sabinis were open to challenges from other gangs and were unable to maintain their domination of the racing scene. At Lewes racecourse in June 1936, a large gang of Hoxton and Islington men set upon a Sabini-protected bookie. Edward Greeno, later to become head of the Flying Squad, describes the incident:

A ringleader of the gang shouted, 'Here they are, boys. Get your tools ready!' And he pulled out a hatchet from under his coat. The whole mob ran at the two men, pulling out weapons as they went: hatchets and hammers, knuckledusters and two-foot iron bars. One man had a length of inch-square rubber and another man's club looked like the half-shaft of a car wrapped in newspaper. Alf had his arms full of bits of gear to build up his stand when the mob smashed at his head with their weapons. He took three or four blows and ran like a hare.

The bookie, Alf Solomons, escaped with minor injuries but his clerk, Mark Frater, was surrounded and would probably have been chopped to pieces had not the police intervened. The police – no doubt through the discreet co-operation of the Sabinis – seem to have had prior knowledge of the attack and were able to round up a considerable number of the Hoxton and Islington men. Sixteen of them were sentenced to long sentences of penal servitude (forty-three and a half years between them) for their revival of racetrack gang warfare. The Sabinis survived but the police now seemed to have gained the upper hand.

The abortive 'Battle of Lewes' attracted considerable press interest and one Sunday newspaper went so far as to profile Darby Sabini – who for fourteen years had carefully kept out of the news – as Britain's leading gangster. Sabini unwisely filed a libel action and – even more unwisely – failed to put in an appearance when the case came to court. Judgement was given against him and he was ordered to pay to pay £775 costs. One might have expected this to be an insignificant sum to someone reputed to earn £20,000–30,000 a year from his racketeering, but Sabini didn't have it, being incapable of saving money – a trait he had in common with the general run of English gangsters. Instead he declared himself bankrupt. This was a bad mistake, as he found himself subjected to detailed enquiries about his income and lifestyle at a public examination. In his circles publicity was not seen as a desirable asset for an active criminal and his prestige was irretrievably damaged. Sabini was no longer able to hold together the Jewish and anti-semitic elements of his gang and, though he and his brothers remained a force, the King's Cross bookmaker 'Big Alf' White was now acknowledged as the dominant figure among the race gangs. However, White, uneasily allied with the more anti-semitic Italians, never achieved more than a local domination and in 1939 he was badly beaten up by a gang of young Stoke Newington tearaways at Harringay Greyhound Stadium. White had three sons to carry on the family business, but with the growing influence of Jack Spot, the days of White domination were numbered.

Spot, who generally gave his real name as Jack Comer, was born in Whitechapel in 1912, the son of Polish Jews who had come to England in the 1890s. Unlike most of the hard-working, law-abiding Jewish East End community, Spot was restless and belligerent ('a fight was better than a good dinner for me') from an early age. By hanging around the local Rowton House and the gyms and boxing clubs where the East End terrors and tearaways congregated, he picked up a style of life very different from that pursued by his brothers and sister employed in tailoring and dressmaking. Having established a reputation as a fearless fighter, he found himself inundated with pleas for protection from Jewish businessmen, bookies, promoters and shopkeepers who felt themselves increasingly vulnerable to anti-semitic violence. In August 1936, when Sir Oswald Mosley attempted to march through the East End, Spot eagerly participated in laying waste his contingent of bodyguards. He was arrested but had the

Jack Spot at the races.

good fortune to come up before a sympathetic Jewish magistrate and got off with a small fine.

From then on he was drawn increasingly into the life of the racetracks and 'spielers', the small illicit gaming clubs widespread throughout Soho and the East End, where the conflict between Jewish and Italian gangs continued to rage. Spot was set upon by a gang of Islington heavies in Foxy's Billiard Hall in Soho in 1938 and badly beaten about the head with billiard cues. But he had the reckless courage of the traditional East End villain and was undeterred by setbacks such as these.

Hardly any record survives of these vicious internecine fights, but Fred Cartwright, a Post Office investigator, stumbled across one in the Café Bleu in Soho and recounts his experience in his autobiography, *G-Men of the GPO*. Sitting upstairs in the café, where he suspected dirty deals involving letters were being hatched, he was disturbed by noises from the basement. Near midnight,

the voices down below began to increase into violence and I noticed an alarmed look on the face of the proprietor, who, I had no doubt, knew his Soho 'boys' pretty intimately. Suddenly he came from behind his counter towards the stairs, evidently with the intention of going below to restore order. But he was too late. There came the unmistakable sound of a general fight. Furniture crashed as chairs were flung about. Glasses were being smashed, and among it all one could hear the 'smack' of fists against flesh. It seemed as though hell was let loose in that basement. The proprietor had descended a few stairs, but he came back in two strides as I heard the sound of

running steps from below. A moment later a man dashed up, his face bleeding from a terrible gash down one cheek. There came another, similarly wounded. These were followed by a veritable pack, several with bruised faces and bleeding noses.

The police tended to turn a blind eye to conflicts within the underworld and intervened only when there seemed a danger of violence spilling over on to the general public. Spot was arrested after a particularly violent affray early in 1939 but was let off with a warning, despite having continued the feud while on remand in Brixton prison by beating up an anti-semitic Italian thug called Antonio Mancini.

Many Italians were interned as enemy aliens when Italy entered the war in 1940, though not the Sabinis. Darby's son served in the RAF and was killed in the Battle of Britain. Darby himself retired to Hove, where he lived quietly until he died in his bed in 1950. Antonio Mancini also slipped through the net, with more troublesome consequences. In May 1941 there was a disturbance at the West End Bridge and Billiards Club in Wardour Street and the Jewish doorman, 'Little Hubby' Distelman, was fatally stabbed. Three Italians were arrested for his murder: Albert Dimes, Joseph Collette and Antonio Mancini. Dimes and Collette were found guilty of unlawful wounding, but the Recorder, Sir Gerald Dodson, decided that 'there was no evidence to show that they did anything more than engage in a rough-and-tumble', and merely bound them over for three years. Mancini had been rather too enthusiastic in his rough and tumbling, however, and he was found guilty of murder. At a time when Britain was fighting for survival, gangland killings appeared inexcusable and at the behest of Scotland Yard, who valued Distelman's brother ('Big Hubby') as an in-former, it was decided to make an example of Mancini. Despite a not unreasonable plea of provocation and self-defence, and an appeal which reached the House of Lords, he was hanged on 31 October 1941.

The man who played too rough: Antonio Mancini, hanged for the murder of 'Little Hubby' Distelman, October 1941.

4 A BURGLAR'S LIFE BETWEEN THE WARS

He moves very slowly and smoothly, rather like a chameleon climbing up a cactus, and he times his movements with natural night noises of the house, putting his foot down as the Grandfather clock ticks. Inside a bedroom, he cocks his ear towards the bed and breathes in tune with one of the sleepers. When he leaves the room he sprinkles a few handfuls of tintacks beside the bed, so that if, by any chance, the sleeping householder should wake and hear something, he won't be able to creep up on the Creep.

Charles Raven, *Underworld Nights* (1956)

Robbing the rich

Protection, prostitution, drug-dealing (along with minor rackets like running fruit machines) were criminal activities only because there was a discrepancy between public demand and legal restriction. At the core of the underworld were the practitioners of the age-old craft of relieving the rich of their valuables. In contrast to the showy flamboyance of the racing gangsters, those who made their living through robbery – burglars, safe-breakers, confidence men, fraudsters, pickpockets and smash and grab bandits – tended to be quiet craftsmen, hardened and sobered by their long years in prison.

The first two decades of the twentieth century saw the summation of the burglar's art as far as private houses were concerned. Skilful, careful crooks like 'Gentleman George' Smithson proved more than a match for the dogs and armed keepers with which the rich defended their country homes. Smithson, dubbed by the newspapers 'King of the Cracksmen', wrote a remarkable account of how he netted hauls of jewels, silver and gold, the value of which would now be reckoned in millions. Smithson had several points in his favour. Unlike most crooks, he kept himself very much apart from the underworld and spent his money discreetly. The son of a prosperous north of England nurseryman, he was well educated and respectably established in a smart Kensington flat with a wife and children who knew nothing about his criminal activities. They did not think to question his nocturnal absences and no one disturbed him in his study, where he spent

The finest country house cracksman: 'Gentleman George' Smithson.

long hours consulting *Debrett's*, *Burke's Landed Gentry* and a comprehensive collection of maps in order to plot the movements of the aristocracy and mark down their stately homes as targets for his depredations.

Smithson's discretion was a considerable asset. As a fellow cracksman explained:

The ordinary crook too often shows his hand by parading his cash and new clothes. It is one of the failings of crookdom to like to be flashy and attract attention. You may be sure that there is always someone lurking about who is prepared to tip the police when an unusual exhibition of wealth is made. Frequently such information leads to a man being pinched on suspicion, and a conviction often follows.

Most of the time Smithson worked alone, travelling to the nearest town or village by train with his trusty bicycle in the guard's van and cycling out to his destination. There he would wait patiently, whatever the weather, until after one o'clock in the morning, when the household was fast asleep and any keepers or watchmen would have made their last patrol, before breaking in. He was always a very cautious burglar, cultivating a nondescript but respectable appearance which allayed suspicion:

Not for me the high-powered motor-car beloved of the novelist. I was a tradesman and I knew, none better, the value of modesty. The bicycle for me every time. It was quiet and unostentatious; I could hide it in the woods while I slunk stealthily towards my destination, recover it when I finished work for the night, and ride away as silently as I had come.

Smithson's sober dress and steady manner helped him when dealing with suspicious village constables and he would consult local directories for a name or two he might work into a story to explain his presence in the area. His respectability also seemed to re-assure guard dogs as to his intentions. While breaking into the rectory at Upton Magna in 1924, he penetrated the rector's study only to discover a big black retriever curled up on an armchair. Deciding that retreat would arouse the dog's suspicions, he decided to go on with his task:

The drawers on the desk were locked. I forced each one of them open and ransacked them one at a time, carefully and systematically. The dog still slept in the chair. In one of the drawers I found a safe key and beside the desk stood the safe. With the same care and precision I opened the safe and rifled that too. The dog mildly snored in unison with my movements. After one final search and one last look round, I patted the dog on the head and commended it for its great faithfulness. It looked up at me in a sleepy canine way, as much as to say, 'Quite all right.' It then turned over and went to sleep again.

Later that night Smithson went on to burgle Altringham Hall, despite the presence of two 'great Alsatian wolfhounds'.

Smithson's troubles came less from carrying out his burglaries than from disposing of his booty. His unwillingness to mix in the underworld and deal with fences meant he had to retain the services of a partner, George Ingram, who was adept at disposing of stolen goods. Ingram was a much more unstable character than Smithson – he endured over two thousand forced feeding sessions during his two-and-a-half-year hunger strike in Dartmoor in the twenties – and his book *Hell's*

Kitchen gives a fascinating but unconvincing alternative interpretation of his relationship with Smithson. He sometimes insisted on accompanying his partner on his nocturnal expeditions in order to guide him towards the sort of valuables his 'buyers' were most willing to accept. Unfortunately he was a noisy and incompetent burglar and on two occasions Ingram's disruption of Smithson's meticulously cautious expeditions led to them being arrested.

Despite his extraordinary success as a burglar, Smithson served three sentences of penal servitude between 1911 and 1929 (when he abandoned his criminal career), which meant that his hundreds of operations had to be concentrated into a mere three and a half years of freedom. When he emerged from Dartmoor in July 1929 the day of the top-class country house burglar was over, but there were still pickings for less sophisticated cracksmen. In his *Spiv's Progress*, John Worby tells how, when on the tramp in the thirties, he met a man who, despite his unprepossessing appearance, was adept at breaking into country houses and making off with anything from lamb chops to priceless heirlooms (which he would bury for a rainy day). Understandably his main target was cash, which he would bank as soon as possible in one of the innumerable accounts he held in different names

An excited housemaid poses for the press the morning after a country house burglary.

Cat burglar caught in the act.

throughout the country. However, the rich were tending to keep their money and valuables in banks and loan their *objets d'art* to museums, and they could live with such pinpricks. More troubling to them was the brief but spectacular phenomenon of the cat burglar.

Cat burglars and creeps

Like muggers in the 1970s or garrotters in the 1860s, cat burglars were something of a media invention. The inherent risks of climbing high buildings and clambering over roofs to reach windows left unlocked because they were considered inaccessible necessarily made this sort of robbery the work of a small and skilful élite. But in the early twenties cat burglar fever gripped the upper-class imagination and all sorts of solutions – loosening drain-pipe fixings, coating them with coloured engine-oil, providing them with steel wire 'cat guards' – were proposed for terminating the 'epidemic'.

At the time the rich were spending longer periods in their town houses than in their country estates and were taking their valuables with them. And as ground floor access to such houses was often impossible, the cat burglar was born. George Ingram, Smithson's erstwhile partner, thought the best time to have a go 'at the climb' was in the early evening, when the occupants of the house were at dinner.

This is a good time, as the ladies don't put on all their jewellery then, but leave full adornment until after dinner, if they are going out. Frequently the jewels are left in the dressing-rooms or bedrooms, and are available for those who are lucky enough to come along at the right time.

The cat burglar who climbed up to the Red Room at Bath House, Piccadilly, in June 1924 made away with jewellery worth anything between £250,000 and £500,000 and there were similar spectacular coups in the late twenties.

Eric Parr's chapter on 'The Climber' in his wonderfully astute underworld compendium, *Grafters All*, stresses:

There has to be a great deal of staff work before the actual robbery can take place. A district is selected in advance, preferably one which has enjoyed a period of immunity and, for two or three days, it's toured by three men in a car (a climbing team is made up of three: the actual climber, a minder and a driver) . . . Finally, they pick out a house with great care. Can it be safely watched for at least three nights in succession? Is there a near-by hiding-place for the car, where it won't be seen by some over-zealous policeman?

Parr didn't think a 'Jacob' was essential:

because every house has its own built-in ladder – the soil-pipe, which always runs close to one of the bedrooms. I stress the word soil-pipe because, contrary to popular belief, no climber risks life, liberty and limb by attempting to climb a rain-pipe secured to the outside wall by short guttering nails. On the other hand, a soil-pipe is firmly held in position by two-and-a-half-inch nails, and will take the weight of any full-grown man.

Burglars have been known to choose particularly difficult targets merely to demonstrate their skills: Mark Benney mentions in his autobiography, *Low Company*, one 'who never gained more than a modest living from his burglaries, and this because he was not so much interested in the proceeds of burglary as in the technique, the art. He burgled as a poet versifies.' Eventually this burglar-poet settled down with a wife and family and went straight. But with nostalgic affection for an art which had become too dangerous for him to practise, he would make nocturnal assaults on his own house, sheepishly returning his loot in the morning. Jim Carstairs, another leading member of the fraternity, tried to construct a philosophical rather than a poetic justification for his activities, insisting that 'thieves are necessary to punish the avaricious and the rich' and that 'law, patriotism, and bodily disease are the real enemies of humanity'.

Most burglars were unconcerned with moral niceties but they were superstitious. Smithson always carried about with him a weird collection of charms, including a heavy iron horseshoe, and criminal raconteur Charles Raven numbered among his friends

Joe Wigram, who insisted that it was lucky to go screwing [i.e burgling] in spats and a straw hat; Barney Newbiggin's brother, Horace, who will never do a house numbered nine or seventeen; Mike Birkbeck, who would go straight home, however hot the tip-off, if he met a Welshman when he was on the way to graft; Blackie Stevens, who swears that dogs can read his thoughts . . .

With these sorts of hang-ups it was not surprising that the majority of burglars chose the most direct and easy form of entrance – a ground-floor or basement window – and were only driven to more risky methods of entry by necessity. Thus cat burglary was always the exception and 'creeping' – the stealthy nocturnal burglary of an occupied house – the most common form of burgling private houses.

Some burglars worked as teams with a 'canary' (a respectable-looking woman who would carry the burglars' tools and take away the stolen goods) and a 'crow' (a look-out). But the common burglar worked alone, using simple implements – a putty knife and a petercane (a small crowbar) – and relied on good luck and his own ability to respond quickly to a situation. Mark Benney, who served an apprenticeship in burglary before becoming a writer, stresses the need to be unobtrusive, to blend into one's surroundings – to wear evening dress, for example, if prowling the streets of Mayfair looking for a likely target. Once in a house, burglary could be a nerve-wracking but thrilling experience. Benney, burgling the St James's Street club where he had worked as a mezzanine valet,

was horribly frightened, and at the same time curiously elated. Slipping quietly through the dark rooms, I had a strange sense of the shadows closing protectively about me, of the rhythms of my being sinking into the silence of small night noises till I became as it were the focal point of a vast brooding darkness.

Creeps would pride themselves on being able to move so silently that sleepers remained undisturbed – according to burglar lore, one had to move when the sleeper breathed out and remain still while he or she breathed in. Such stealth was unknown to country house cracksmen like Smithson, who felt comfortable only in big houses, where the night-time creaking and groaning masked the noise he made. In a big country house, 'Windows rattle, floors give a sudden crack, mice scurry round the wainscotting. Trees rustle outside', and consequently sleepers were less sensitive to untoward noises in the night.

Robbery was dealt with severely by the courts in the twenties and thirties, unlike inter-criminal violence. For example, men found guilty of race gang violence rarely suffered sentences longer than six months – after all, they were only harming men of their own kind – and many leading racing gangsters, including Darby Sabini and Jack Spot, managed to avoid custodial sentences entirely. In contrast, a burglar caught with his tools after nine o'clock at night could, if regarded as a habitual offender, be sent away for a long sentence of preventive detention. Robbery with violence brought sentences of at least three or four years and a flogging with the cat-o'-nine-tails, which left one scarred for life. Even successful burglars like Smithson could expect to spend a large proportion of their lives in prison.

Billy Hill, a very different character to Smithson, was successful enough to emerge as 'Boss of Britain's Underworld' in the fifties, but spent fourteen of what might have been the best years of his life, between 1930 and 1950, behind bars. He was born in 1911 in

A young Billy Hill (second from right) with his first gang.

Seven Dials, then a last remnant of the old St Giles rookery rather than a fashionable intersection between Covent Garden and the West End. His mother was 'a buyer of bent gear', his father 'had five or six cons for belting cozzers' and most of the twenty-one little Hills who survived adolescence turned to one aspect of crime or another. After moving to Netley Street in Camden Town, Billy began work as a grocer's delivery boy, with a lucrative sideline in feeding his brother-in-law information about likely targets for burglaries. Before long he was doing his own break-ins.

Hill took to 'drumming', the quick ransacking of a house in the owner's absence, rather than the riskier and more skilful practice of 'creeping'. This was an increasing trend of the inter-war years, prompted partly by the expansion of accessible suburban housing and partly by the fact that daytime breaking and entering (between the hours of 6 a.m. and 9 p.m.) was treated much more leniently by the courts than night-time burglary (between the hours of 9 p.m. and 6 a.m.). For the low-to-middle-ranking burglar, middle-class houses were to provide a modestly profitable hunting ground, but more ambitious crooks turned away from private houses to the vaults and safes of banks, building societies, offices, cinemas and restaurants, where an increasingly large part of the nation's loose change was stored in the inter-war years.

The heyday of the safe-breaker

Safe-breaking required the sort of skill, co-ordination and craftsmanship which had characterized the country house burglar. Most big jobs were carried out by teams of men: a driver, a look-out man, the safe-breaker and his assistant, and a couple of men to force an entrance and if necessary deal with the night-watchman. Often the safe-breaker would be brought in only for the actual robbery and would have nothing to do with the planning of the operation or the disposal of the goods. Eddie Browne, an early 'road-pirate' (smash and grab robber) who began his career in serious crime as a safe-breaker's assistant, makes the point that his boss 'was usually employed by the crooks only to open a safe. He had nothing to do with breaking into a place or even with the arrangements.' He would only be appointed when a target had been decided on, and his tools would be ready and waiting for him on the job. All he had to do was turn up – and open the safe. However, Eddie Chapman, one of the most successful safe-breakers of the thirties, reckoned that thirty-eight of the forty-five jobs he later admitted to were carried out by himself alone. Chapman favoured cinemas, dance-halls and department stores, where significant amounts of ready cash could be found, but he had good enough underworld contacts to make it worth his while to steal the contents of jewellers' and furriers' safes too.

Chapman came from a respectable middle-class family (his father was a chief engineer, albeit one reduced to working as a Sunderland pub landlord during the Depression) and he had joined the Coldstream Guards at seventeen. However, on his first leave he was seduced by a woman of easy virtue and rapidly drawn into the underworld. Like Jim Phelan, the IRA gunman whose stories of underworld life offer the best insight into the criminal ethos of the inter-war years, Chapman combined considerable intellectual gifts with a 'wideness', an amoral contempt for the hypocrisies of the law-abiding classes, which won him acceptance among criminals. After a brief sojourn in Lewes gaol for his involvement in a smash and grab raid he teamed up with a top-class safe-breaker and soon learnt enough to pursue a solo career. Lock technology had advanced to the point that it was rare indeed for a burglar to be able to pick the lock or work out the combination of a safe. But the safe-breaker had a new weapon in his arsenal – gelignite.

Gelignite, unlike the highly unstable nitro-glycerine favoured by American crooks, was safe enough to handle but great skill was required in calculating the amount to be used for each individual safe. Too little damaged the keyhole, making it difficult to insert a second charge, but left the safe unopened; too much blew the safe and its contents to smithereens – and the safe-breaker too, if he was unlucky. Chapman was wily enough to test the effects of his explosions – initially on trees, later on specially purchased second-hand safes. A certain amount of danger also surrounded the insertion of a detonator into the bed of gelignite because often its circumference needed to be reduced before it could be inserted into the keyhole of a safe. According to one old professional, the best way of doing this was for the safe-breaker to crimp it between his teeth – an extremely delicate operation. Too much pressure meant disaster both to the operator and to those around him. 'So he crimps the small cylinder very carefully and when he's satisfied that he's reduced it sufficiently, he eases it into its final resting place.' Once the gelignite and detonator had been safely packed into the keyhole it would be sealed with plasticine or, in Chap-

man's case, chewing gum. The safe would be draped in curtains, carpets and whatever else could be found to muffle the explosion and the wires from the detonator connected to a battery at a safe distance. If the operation was a success there would be a dull thud and the door to the safe would swing open.

Safe-breakers who worked as part of a team usually expected the gang boss to supply them with gelignite and detonators. Chapman, who preferred to work outside the London area, stole his own from isolated quarries, and worked only with men he chose himself. Even so, he was eventually caught

A successfully blown safe.

when one of his helpers sent a bottle of scent to an untrustworthy girlfriend, thus inadvertently revealing to the police Chapman's Jersey hideout. Before he was rounded up, he robbed the safe of the Palm Beach Casino, a local dance-hall, and instead of being returned to England for trial on a long string of charges, he was given a two-year sentence in a Jersey gaol. By the time he was released in October 1941, the island was under German occupation, and Chapman launched himself on a successful career as a double agent. He returned to England as a German spy and won the gratitude of the British authorities, some useful contacts in the Special Branch and a pardon for his forty-five safe-breaking offences in exchange for feeding false information to his German spymasters.

Motor bandits

Between the wars the population of Britain remained stagnant while the number of cars increased from 200,000 in 1919 to 2 million in 1939. As A. J. P. Taylor put it, 'The Baby Austin ousted the baby. The nursery gave place to the garage.' Car theft and the use of cars as getaway vehicles prompted the formation of Scotland Yard's Flying Squad in 1919. Initially the Squad had only a couple of lookout vans but it soon proved its effectiveness. Before long the underworld was complaining about the unfairness of tactics like 'using little eight horse-power Morris vans with big Bentley engines inside them'. The Squad expanded rapidly and with the adoption of radio control became an effective

force for the inner London area. But crooks were quick to use the motor-car as a means of extending their activities to new pastures.

George Smithson eschewed the use of a car but on one occasion his partner persuaded him to experiment with a motorcycle. Unfortunately it was a thoroughly unreliable machine and it was only through the help of a friendly and unsuspicious policeman that Smithson managed to reach his destination. He burgled Benham Park, between Bath and Chippenham, and made off with two Gainsborough portraits, but punctures and mechanical breakdowns plagued his getaway and he finished up returning to London by train. Smithson's reliance on trains, particularly when descending late at night on a small country station or waiting for an early morning train with the proceeds of the previous night's burglary in his bag, involved him in uncomfortably risky situations. The use of a car would have enabled him to avoid contact with suspicious station-masters and ticket collectors, but cars made a lot of noise and were as yet still rare enough to attract the attention of village policemen. One of the most celebrated murder cases of the twenties, the cold-blooded killing of PC Gutteridge, occurred when the intrepid Gutteridge stopped a car in a quiet Essex lane and was shot by the two car thiefs when he attempted to question them as to what they were doing in the area.

The case attracted a considerable amount of attention because Gutteridge had had both his eyes shot out. His murderers – caught because of a minor traffic accident in Neepsend, Sheffield, by one of Percy Sillitoe's constables – turned out to be a good-natured but easily led grammar-school boy, William Henry Kennedy, and a psychopathic second-hand car salesman, Frederick Guy Browne. Each accused the other of the policeman's murder and both were hanged. But for those in the underworld, at least, it was obvious that Browne was the murderer and that, in the tradition of a Victorian melodrama villain, he had shot out the policeman's eyes because he feared they reflected the image of the man who had killed him.

The crooked second-hand car trade was already flourishing by the mid-twenties and continued to expand until 1939, when petrol rationing knocked the bottom out of the market for second-hand cars. Two main types of car theft existed. The first was the snatching of cars by crooks for use as getaway vehicles. Eddie Browne, like most motor bandits, insisted on using a stolen car for his smash and grab raids, but Billy Hill and his gang preferred to hire a car for theirs. The second type of theft was the more elaborate stealing of cars for re-sale to the public. This entailed the doctoring of log books and the changing of engine and chassis numbers as well as the paraphernalia of respraying and false number plates, and became a highly organized business in the thirties.

The happiest hunting grounds for the motor-assisted burglar were the suburbs inhabited by the middle classes, where policemen patrolled only infrequently, gardens provided excellent cover and large windows offered easy points of entry. Here, where there was a relatively high population of cars, the motorized burglar was much less likely to be noticed and the car provided a convenient means of carrying away the fruits of robbery. But such discreet, unobtrusive – and increasingly common – forms of burglary attracted less attention than the spectacular exploits of the 'motor bandits', the most famous of whom were Ruby Sparks and the 'Bobbed-Haired Bandit'.

Sparks, like Billy Hill, was born into a criminal family, in Tiger Yard, Bermondsey. His mother had a considerable local reputation as a buyer of (stolen) gold and silver, and his father, a horse coper, one as a fighter who used to pickle his knuckles in brine 'so that his fists were black and hard as fairground shyballs'. Ruby began his criminal life working with three local villains who would pack him up in a hamper and despatch him on to mail trains. He would emerge from his hiding place and steal registered letters. When his mentors were caught during a warehouse robbery, Ruby worked on his own as a cat burglar, acquiring his nickname at an early stage in his career from a robbery he carried out in Park Lane.

Entering the house, he broke into a desk and found a box of red stones which he pocketed. After being informed by a 'buyer' that such large and perfect stones must necessarily be 'jargoons' (artificial), he gave them away to anyone curious enough to want one, only to discover the next day that he had burgled the London home of an Indian maharajah and the stones he had so carelessly disposed of were uncut rubies worth £40,000. Despite this embarrassing start to his career he became a skilful and successful cat burglar, but, on teaming up with the 'Bobbed-Haired Bandit', he turned to the less

The unfortunate PC Gutteridge.

His murderer, Frederick Guy Browne.

The scene of the crime: Howe Green, Essex.

subtle but equally lucrative art of the smash and grab raid.

Breaking plate-glass windows was not so easy as it might seem and became a highly specialized underworld skill, the best-known exponent of which was an illiterate but intelligent character known as Corey Moggs. According to Jim Phelan, Moggs used his hammer so effectively that the gangs he was associated with stole something like £180,000 in the inter-war period. Sparks's initial attempts were less successful: 'I wrapped a brick in brown paper to look like a neat parcel and threw it at Catchpole and William's window. Then I had a bad surprise, for the brick parcel bounced right off the window and whizzed past my ear.' He tried twice more before giving up, fortunately without anybody in the crowded street working out what he was trying to do. 'They could not have twigged it was a brick and perhaps thought I had succumbed to an impulse to hurl my packet of dinner sandwiches at the window.' After several more practice runs he developed a more effective technique and claimed that he could knock the right-sized hole in any thickness of glass: 'One tap for testing – two taps to make the hole – a quick grab and we were away.' This had the unfortunate side-effect of showering him with splinters of glass, so that his wrists and arms 'looked as if I'd fought ten rounds with a lawnmower'. He used Bulldog clips to hold the gashes shut until the 'Bobbed-Haired Bandit' could stitch them up for him'.

Cruder smash and grab men relied on very large lumps of concrete, though this method had the disadvantage of making such a mess of the window that it was difficult to pick out the rings and jewellery from the debris. On the other hand, a professional like Moggs could tap fifteen holes in the window with a platelayer's hammer, push in the glass and throw it out again on to the pavement within fifteen seconds. Speed was essential, as, if the raid could be carried off in under a minute, passers-by tended to be too shocked to react.

The main danger was in making a getaway through a network of often busy streets and bold, adventurous driving was at a premium. Sparks's partner and driver, Lilian Goldstein, the 'Bobbed-Haired Bandit', acquired an almost mythical reputation in the twenties. Newspapers described her as, 'A girl bandit with dark bobbed hair, a small innocent-looking face and an active and intelligent brain', and reported, 'She is often dressed in a red beret and motoring coat of the same colour, or in an all-green motoring outfit, and she is believed to be the "brains" behind recent country-house raids.' 'Nutty' Sharpe of the Flying Squad had first-hand experience of her and noted, 'She usually drove a big Mercedes car. Sitting at the wheel with a man's raincoat collar turned up around her close-fitting little black hat, there wasn't much of her to see.' He regarded her as 'a very spunky girl ... trusted by these very dangerous criminals as one who would submit to anything rather than give away any secrets of the gang'. In reality she was a respectable lower-middle-class Jewish girl who had drifted into crime after an unhappy love affair with a married man. Cool, determined and resourceful, she was unperturbed

Smash and grab!

by the very male ethos of the underworld, and was able to command respect for her speed, ingenuity and aggression as a getaway driver.

For a five-year period she and Sparks carried out their raids successfully and it was only in 1927, when increasing pressure from the Flying Squad persuaded them to return to cat burglary and country house robbery, that they were caught. As there was no proof of their involvement in smash and grab raids, the 'Bobbed-Haired Bandit' was acquitted and Sparks escaped relatively lightly with three years' penal servitude.

A burglar's tool kit.

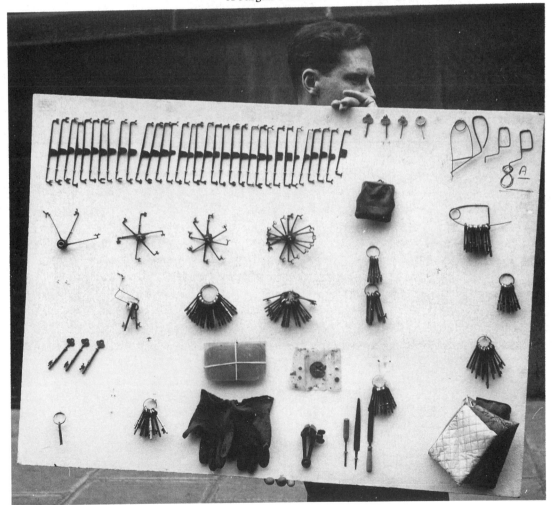

5 PRISON CULTURE

The prison is an intricate, elaborate community of a unique kind, with laws, customs, hierarchies, rewards, punishments, and motives as different as can be conceived from those prevailing in the outside world. It is a difficult world for the ordinary human being to acclimatize himself to, demanding constant vigilance and control. The faculties it exercises most are those least useful in the world outside; and conversely, those most useful in the outer world are the ones positively prohibited here.

Mark Benney, *Gaol Delivery* (1948)

The evolution of the English prison

Prison culture was essentially a product of the nineteenth century. Until the reforms of the 1790s, most criminal offences were punishable by death and the small prison population was made up of a promiscuous collection of debtors, prostitutes, child criminals and people awaiting trial. New philosophies professing a belief in human perfectability and social progress brought about a change in attitude towards criminals and crime. Criminals were no longer seen as useless pests to be exterminated as perfunctorily as possible; they were misguided individuals who could be reclaimed for society once a proper respect for religion and a willingness to learn industrious habits had been instilled.

Reformers like John Howard and Jeremy Bentham argued that scientific methods could be applied to turn criminals into obedient, law-abiding, hard-working citizens. In Bentham's words, 'rogues could be ground honest'. They stipulated that criminals must be kept from contaminating each other with their malicious habits, be provided with hard, laborious, monotonous and unrewarding work to get them used to the rigours of industrial labour, and be kept in solitude in order to meditate on and come to terms with their sins. In 1842 a new prison was built at Pentonville, modelled on Bentham's 'Panopticon' or Inspection House. Double rows of cells radiated outwards from a central hall like spokes from the hub of a wheel, so that each prisoner was kept isolated and under constant surveillance from his gaolers. This 'radial' type of prison became the model for

over fifty local prisons built over the next ten years and it was around these buildings that the modern English prison system was shaped. Prisoners were kept in solitary confinement and worked in their cells, picking oakum, grinding bones for glue, sewing mailbags or doing a specified number of turns on the hand-crank. When contact between prisoners was unavoidable, they were made to wear masks which made communication impossible. Such isolation, it was hoped, would give the convict ample time to reflect on his wicked and useless life and make him turn away from crime.

Reduction in the number of offences punishable by death in the late eighteenth century might have caused an explosion of the prison population had it not been for the growing practice of sentencing criminals to periods of transportation to the colonies – generally for seven or fourteen years, and sometimes for life. Transportation to America dated back to Elizabethan times but it had been on a relatively small scale (America could rely on black slaves and poor immigrants for its cheap labour) and had anyway been terminated by the Declaration of Independence in 1776. Thus it was Australia, a vast, empty, faraway land which attracted few free migrants, that became the main dumping ground for British convicts. In the first half of the nineteenth century around 150,000 British undesirables were exported, but after 1840 most of the Australian states decided that convicts were more trouble than they were worth and closed their doors. Tasmania and Western Australia accepted convicts for another few years, but by the 1860s transportation was no longer a viable solution and Britain had to make proper provision for its convicts at home.

The new prisons were built to house short-term prisoners – even a year or two of total isolation was having the unforeseen side-effect of driving men mad. Convicts serving long sentences had to be dealt with differently. In 1849 Major-General Sir Joshua Jebb instituted a system of 'penal servitude' which would replace 'the lost opportunities of the bush and the outback' by setting up what amounted to labour camps. Offenders who previously would have been liable for transportation served out their sentences toiling on public works – digging out the great dock basins at Chatham, building the breakwater at Portland and reclaiming the boggy land of High Dartmoor for farming. Prisoners were banded together into work parties but were forbidden to speak to prevent them from 'contaminating' one another. Those who attempted to do so were given a spell of solitary confinement and a bread and water diet in the punishment cells. Nevertheless, convicts quickly learnt the ventriloquist's skill of speaking without moving the lips. Jim Phelan, the IRA gunman sentenced to life imprisonment for his part in a raid on a Liverpool post office in 1923, found the silent rule still enforced but effectively subverted. On arriving at Maidstone convict prison in 1923, he was fascinated by the noise of the returning work gangs:

There was a strange susurration which I could not locate or identify. It was rather like the murmuring sound made by the wings of a thousand starlings when they are ganging up in the autumn. I was hearing the 'silent system' of the English convict prisons for the first time ... That bird's-wing whisper was the 'Stir Bat', the lip-still murmur which no bread-and-water-giving warder can legally describe as talking.

The ability to communicate effectively through the rich but economical argot of the underworld tended to mark off the 'wide people' inside for various forms of fraud or robbery from the 'steamers', who, generally because of some ill-thought-out attempt at murder or rash indulgence in sexual deviance, found themselves unexpectedly plummeted into the underworld.

Between the wars the prison population fell. Convictions for criminal offences hardly increased and judicial sentences became marginally less harsh. For most of the inter-war period the number of convicts serving a sentence of three or more years' penal servitude was less than two thousand. Portland prison, 'a great fortress-like structure of stone, built on a solid foundation of rock, rising like some gargantuan monster of the deep from the turbulent seas around it', was turned into a Borstal in the early twenties after its large contingent of Sinn Fein prisoners was released or removed to other prisons. Camp Hill, built a few hundred yards from Parkhurst on the Isle of Wight, was opened in 1912 to house criminals sentenced to preventive detention but was converted into a Borstal in 1935. Apart from the women's prison at Holloway, which housed prisoners serving anything from a few weeks to life, convicts serving long sentences were concentrated at Maidstone, Parkhurst and Dartmoor.

Maidstone was reserved for first offenders (known as 'stars'), Parkhurst for those not 100 per cent physically or mentally fit and Dartmoor for hardened recidivists. Of the three prisons, Parkhurst was by far the best, though there was a period in the late twenties under the baleful governorship of Colonel Hales when it was considered the toughest gaol in Europe. Maidstone tended to have a milder and more lenient regime, but unlike Parkhurst and Dartmoor, where convicts worked on farms and forests around the prison, there was no possibility of work outside the prison walls, and the company was less congenial. The high percentage of sex cases and reprieved murderers tended to create a servile, back-stabbing ethos, made worse in the twenties by Captain Stephenson ('Stinker Stephen'), the vindictive and unsavoury governor.

Jim Phelan hated it and was almost relieved when he was transferred to Dartmoor as a potential mutineer:

There is no hollow veneer of culture, no empty prattle of prison reform at the Moor. This is a place where the convict gangs are held at forced labour, under the musket and cutlass and club . . . The change from the mean, small, false stuffiness of Maidstone was startling. This place was tough – tough till it hurt. But at least the warders and officials didn't pretend that it was some sort of training school or a course in civics.

Phelan is one of the very few prison writers to have anything good to say about Dartmoor. After the confines of Maidstone, he found a sort of awesome dignity about a prison containing 600 hardened criminals shut away on the wilds of Dartmoor. At night,

it really was very beautiful, for a while. No ship in mid-ocean at midnight ever approached it, no empty house, no cemetery. Here was a huge granite structure teeming with life, with hundreds of men packed close to one another in nine-foot niches in the wall, where the squeak of a mouse sounded like the roar of a whole starving zoo.

But for all his admiration for Captain Morgan, the stern but fair governor, and his satisfaction at plying a useful trade in the blacksmith's shop, the grim hopelessness of life on the Moor made Phelan desperate enough to plan an escape. And when that failed he exacerbated his asthma in order to get himself transferred to Parkhurst.

Dartmoor had been used for American and French prisoners of war in the late eighteenth century but had lain derelict for half a century before being cleaned up and opened as a convict prison in 1850. Its forbidding setting and gloomy atmosphere threw men into the depths of depression. Parkhurst was better. The original building had been a shooting lodge for Queen Victoria's father and the prison complex had grown up higgledy-piggledy around it – prison halls, workshops, a hospital. Its position on a steep hill further emphasized its irregularity and difference from the severely geometrical radial prisons favoured by the Victorians. But for most of the twenties the presence of a bullying and incompetent governor meant that life at Parkhurst was so bad that prisoners petitioned to be transferred to Dartmoor.

The nature of prison officials was of vital importance to the well-being of the prisoners, who observed them closely:

Inside Parkhurst.

A new screw is watched as no convict ever was watched even in the heyday of the gaolmakers! His every mannerism and tiny habit are recorded, passed on, told to newcomers. His category is fixed, be he Bleedn Gent or Bitches Basterd. His cough, his wink, his snort, even the morning colour of his eyes and his changing smell are talked of and re-talked until he is known from his boot-heels to the centre of his solar plexus.

He would then be ranked in a descending hierarchy from 'Bleedn Gent', 'Bleedn Good', 'Thumbs Up', 'All Right', through 'Not Bad', 'a Bit Crooked', to 'Wicked', a 'Basterd', a 'Bitches Basterd', and 'Bleedn Murder'. Kindness to convicts could cost a warder dear.

'Fraternization' between prisoners and warders was frowned upon and was liable to result in the warder being handed a 'half-sheet' – a half-sheet of foolscap upon which he would be asked to explain his alleged dereliction of duty. Too many half-sheets could result in dismissal, and as gaolers lived in tied houses, loss of job would also involve loss of home.

Warders' wages were low and there tended to be little solidarity between the ex-servicemen, who recieved small but significant sums as reservists, and warders drawn from 'prison families', which were particularly common on the Isle of Wight and Dartmoor, where the tradition of prison service stretched back for generations. Phelan preferred the ex-servicemen, who had seen a bit of life, to the Moormen and Islanders, with their inbuilt hostility and contempt for the convicts whose lives they shared. 'The men who had seen the world, who had fought, known death and torment at close quarters, had no predisposition for cruelty-pleasure at the expense of helpless men. There was something like a war between them and the medieval type.' Phelan thought that the better type of warder was winning out over the 'slinking smart-aneefishunts', except in the case of Dartmoor, but he could hardly be expected to have foreseen the post-war explosion in the prison population which was to increase tension between warders and prisoners.

The height of ambition for a prison warder was to be appointed, after many years of service, as the Chief Officer (the 'Chief Screw'). Governors and deputy governors were rarely appointed from within the prison

service and tended to be ex-military and naval officers. They varied from unimaginative but scrupulously fair disciplinarians like Captain Morgan, who ran Dartmoor in the mid-twenties, to lamentably unsuitable types such as Colonel Hales, who was in charge of Parkhurst during the same period. Hales emerges from Phelan's prison memoirs as a bullying buffoon:

He strode around Parkhurst, like Ajax defying the lightning, knowing that the vile, terrible murderers and burglars were quailing as he passed, knowing that they were only restrained from raping servant-girls on Parkhurst main road, and from murdering the errand-boys on Rockwood Avenue, because he, Hales, was there to hold the desperate monsters down ... He stode everywhere, and there is only one phrase to describe his gait. Hales walked about like a small boy playing pirates. He took a tremendous pace, and his shoulders went from side to side like a sailing-ship pitching in a heavy sea.

Other prison writers, like Val Davis, the 'Mayfair gangster' who spent half his ten-year sentence in Parkhurst, and Wilfred Macartney, who spent eight years there as a 'Communist spy', are even more scathingly contemptuous. By 1930 Parkhurst was on the verge of a mutiny, but the Prison Commission had the sense to replace Hales with the most interesting governor of the inter-war years, Captain Gerold Fancourt Clayton.

Clayton was the son of a prison governor and was born and brought up within a prison environment. But perhaps because of his experiences during the war – where he lost an ear and had his shoulder smashed – he had an unusually humane approach. When he took over at Parkhurst, he commented he was, 'succeeding a man who believed always in the sternest discipline possible, while I on the contrary believed in producing as normal an atmosphere as possible'. This didn't mean that he was soft. Macartney, who nicknamed him 'Old One Lug', comments with annoyance on his passion for symmetry, which meant that cells had to be meticulously tidied, but he acknowledges Clayton's attempts to stop the routine beating up of troublesome prisoners and his willingness to listen to prisoners' complaints. Phelan and Macartney both won concessions from him – a chess club, a gramophone, a Christmas dinner of sausages, eggs and bacon – and, at the risk of antagonizing his staff, Clayton reorganized the kitchens so that, for a time at least, food was cooked properly and the endemic pilfering of prison food stopped.

Before his spell at Parkhurst, Clayton had done a three-year stint at Maidstone (succeeding Stephenson) and two years at Dartmoor (succeeding Morgan). In 1935, when he left Parkhurst as the most experienced and most popular governor in the prison service, he might have expected to have been appointed to the Prison Commission. Instead he was sent to Wandsworth for four years and suffered a minor mental breakdown. From Wandsworth he moved to Brixton, but during the Blitz he had a recurrence of his mental troubles and had to resign from the service. Such was the dismal end to the career of a man who tried to see the prisoners' point of view and ameliorate the conditions in which they served their sentences.

Clayton's autobiography, *The Walls Are Strong*, makes interesting reading, but the real measure of his achievement is the guarded but undeniably warm tribute paid to him by the likes of Phelan, Macartney and Ruby Sparks. Phelan, pointing out that he was the only governor or deputy governor he came across in his thirteen years inside who understood gaol jargon, comments that 'he might have done a life-lagging so well did he know and understand and sympathize with the convict mind'. Sparks describes him as 'tall and stringy-looking, with a face like a bad-tempered stoat'. But it was Clayton who persuaded him to do his lagging quietly and avoid the punishment cells, and the as yet unreformed smash and grab bandit came to visit him in Wandsworth to thank him for his help. Macartney, a Communist contemptuous of the society Clayton worked to uphold, nevertheless granted him a heartfelt eulogy:

For the half-wit, the irresponsible, and those who had definitely suffered ill and wicked treatment, such as the Dartmoor mutineers, he had more than a soft spot; he had a deep understanding, and nothing, not all the ravings of the rigid disciplinarians, would make him depart from his line of attempting, within the range of his competency, to give these men a fair and even break.

Discipline and punishment

In 1922, Alexander Paterson, a determined advocate of reform was appointed as one of the three Prison Commissioners (though he was never to become chairman). Paterson believed that the only deterrent part of a prison sentence should be the disgrace of appearing in a public court and the loss of a prisoner's liberty, and that the prison regime should be designed to train the convict to become a good citizen. Captain Clayton thought him in too much of a hurry to 'thrust his ultra-modern ideas' on 'an old-fashioned, dingy, quite inadequate prison administration' and complained that when introducing new ideas he made little attempt to explain them to his staff, who consequently failed to carry them out properly. There is little doubt of Paterson's sincerity, and where he was able to start from scratch, as in the Borstal system for young offenders, he was able to initiate a number of bold and progressive experiments. But the prison system remained stubbornly immune to change.

This was partly because of the dead weight of Victorian prison buildings. New ideas needed new buildings to suit them and, with the exception of Camp Hill, a centre for hardened recidivists serving sentences of preventive detention, no new prisons were built between the 1860s and the 1950s. The nature of the buildings tended to determine that of the prison. In Pentonville and the smaller prisons modelled on it, prison life was centred on the individual cell and there was no provision for association between prisoners during work or leisure hours. When workshops and canteens were added they tended to be cramped and poorly sited. Reforms which allowed prisoners to eat, work and even attend concerts and evening classes together were resisted by gaolers, who spent so much time locking and unlocking heavy steel doors that they resented any 'inessen-

tial' movement of prisoners from their cells. Of the three main convict stations – Maidstone, Parkhurst and Dartmoor – Maidstone was old and small and restricted by its town-centre site; Dartmoor streamed with damp most of the year and was often cut off by snow during the winter; and only the sprawling, unplanned complex of buildings at Parkhurst was in the least adaptable. Thus progress and reform tended to be more illusory than real. The no-talking rule was gradually phased out, but as one articulate convict recalled, talking was permitted only at the whim of the discipline warders. 'You might exchange a few remarks with a neighbour, and then hear the warder shout: "That'll be enough talking!" If you continued, you'd be for it, not for talking but for "disobeying an order by continuing to talk when ordered to stop".' More prisoners were punished for 'talking offences' than for anything except trafficking in tobacco until the mid-forties.

Clayton and a handful of other humane governors did their best to run their prisons fairly, but they had few illusions about reforming the inmates. Mark Benney reckoned that a good governor interpreting the rules fairly and extending as much sympathy as possible to the prisoners 'can never make of a prison anything but a bitter, meaningless little world of isolation'. And this sense of prison as a harsh, alien world desolatingly isolated from the real world outside appears repeatedly in the prison autobiographies of the inter-war years. Wilfred Macartney, who wrote *Walls Have Mouths*, the most illuminating account of prison life between the wars, was an ex-army officer from a one-time wealthy family, and he was struck by the degrading way he was now treated as a convict:

That the convict belongs to another biological species is the characteristic belief of the official. And to strengthen this conception the convict is treated unnaturally: he is fed with strange food, must wear weird clothes, must not speak, must go to bed at a ridiculous hour, and is treated like an animate tool. The distance that separates the governor of a gaol from a convict is fathomless.

Not all convicts meekly accepted their degradation. Macartney's Marxism stood him in good stead: expecting no mercy from his 'class enemies', he was able to fight the system with a dogged rationalism which eventually paid off. Jim Phelan's archaic but indomitable belief in 'manliness' led him to risk a bread and water regime by addressing the prison 'heads' as equals, saying, for example, 'Good morning' rather than standing stiffly to attention. But he was thought to be 'as cunning as a sackful of weasels' as well as being a good blacksmith, and he was generally able to steer clear of confrontation. Like the 'wide men' of the gaol – the professional thieves, robbers, confidence tricksters and fraudsters of the underworld, who regarded the prison as an occupational hazard – he was able to work out a *modus vivendi* with prison officers pleased to work with men who understood (if they didn't necessarily obey) the unwritten as well as the written rules of the gaol.

Prison culture was a mixture of underworld codes and practices (its language, for example) and authoritarian patterns imposed from above. Prisoners tended to mix with their own kind – burglars with burglars, paedophiles with paedophiles, for example –

but they were officially categorized by the number of offences they had committed and how much of their sentence they had served. Convicts were divided into three classes: stars, intermediates and recidivists. Stars were first offenders, though this could include both someone convicted of a relatively minor crime and a reprieved murderer, a naïve first offender and a dyed-in-the-wool professional who had 'fallen' after several years of dishonest endeavour. Stripes, ordinaries or intermediates were those convicted of more than one offence; and recidivists were continual reoffenders, though again this category embraced those guilty of petty crimes like stealing from church offertory boxes and the genuinely hardened bank robber or smash and grab bandit such as Billy Hill or Ruby Sparks.

The Prison Commission made some attempt to keep the different categories apart. Maidstone's population was largely made up of stars, Dartmoor's of recidivists. Parkhurst housed stars, intermediates and recidivists, but attempts were made to keep them separate. There was a certain irony, however, in the concern of the authorities to keep stars convicted of incest, rape, child murder and various forms of sadism from being corrupted by habitual bank robbers and burglars.

A more real distinction between prisoners was in terms of 'stages'. For the first eighteen months of a sentence a prisoner was in First Stage, a condition with few privileges. With a year and a half of good conduct behind him he moved up to Second Stage, and after a further year to Third Stage, when the number of books, letters and visits he could

'Chokey', the formidable Parkhurst punishment block.

receive was increased and he was allowed an hour of 'talking exercise' every other evening. Finally, if he managed to keep out of trouble for four years, he passed into Special Stage and joined the privileged élite of the prison. He was now paid sixpence a day for his work and was able to buy tobacco and other luxuries.

The prison authorities used Stage privileges as a means of enforcing discipline, and Macartney argues convincingly that the carrot of increasing privileges was more effective than the stick administered in the punishment cells. But the prison authorities insisted on combining the two and always imposed corporal or dietary punishment as well. Prisoners were disciplined for various small infringements, for offences involving tobacco and other contraband, for talking (or rather refusing to obey an order to stop talking), for insolence, for fighting, for attempting to escape. Attacking a warder, along with mutiny and 'incitement to mutiny', generally brought a flogging.

There were two punishment diets. Number One could be imposed for only fifteen days at a time and consisted of bread and water. Number Two was bread, porridge and potatoes, and it could be imposed for as long as forty-two days. The effects on a prisoner already poorly nourished from the ordinary prison diet could be startling. Ruby Sparks spent a great deal of time in the punishment cells and became very hungry:

At Dartmoor I had chewed away nearly all my wooden table in the punishment cell. Ate it, mouthful by mouthful, swallowing the chewed pulp of splinters to fill out my empty stomach. The table wasn't anything particularly tasty. It was just a scrubbed wooden ledge, soggy from years of Dartmoor's eternal dampness. Its flavour was soap and firewood. But I'd eaten it. The lot!

It did him little good. The unsympathetic governor, A. N. Roberts, awarded him another fourteen days and put him in a cell with a metal table.

Apart from starvation the other main disadvantage of solitary confinement was the interminable boredom of being stuck in a cold bare cell with nothing to do. In local prisons cell tasks would be provided, but this could make life even more unpleasant. Billy Hill, caught trying to escape from Wandsworth in 1927, was made to pound bones in the punishment cells:

The stench of the decaying bones was vile. Then I got used to that, because once or twice I was sick and when I did spew I hurt my stomach. I was sick all over myself. I knocked my body against the cubicle. It was uncomfortable when I was sick. So I was not sick any more.

Some particularly recalcitrant prisoners served the whole of their sentences in 'chokey', having been caught in a repetitive cycle of bitterness and resentment, violence and punishment. A prisoner would be returned from the punishment cells half-starved and half-deranged and before long would vent his fury by smashing up everything in his cell, whereupon he would punished again. Resistance offered to angry warders might well be followed by an unofficial beating up and an official flogging.

The grisly ritual of a flogging with the cat-o'-nine-tails became increasingly rare after 1935 and was abolished entirely by the 1948 Criminal Justice Act. But for most of the inter-war period it was a regular occurrence in the life of a gaol. The guilty man would be brought from the punishment cells when the other convicts were at work, stripped to the waist and strapped to the flogging triangle, his head fixed so that he would not be able to turn it and see who was flogging him. The 'basher' was expected to aim his blows an inch below the shoulder blade and three inches above the waist-line, but accuracy was very variable. The first three blows were the vital ones and if a man could withstand them he would usually absorb the rest without too much distress. Macartney was told by the old lags of Parkhurst that it was better to howl: 'You might upset the governor – especially if he's a boozer, and therefore a bit nervy – and he may order the flogger to stop.' But he avoided the cat and so never put the theory to the test.

Some prisoners were able to laugh off a flogging (though their backs would be scarred for life), while others attempted suicide rather than face the ordeal. To escape it entirely prisoners had to avoid situations which brought them into conflict with the authorities, though this meant an almost superhuman stoicism:

Nowhere more than in gaol is the penalty for losing one's head so severe. Thousands of times, in an ordinary sentence, the convict has to display a stoicism beside which the fiction-Indian calm is as the excitement of a dancing dervish. Again and again I have seen men lose their most treasured possessions, under the eyes of a watching warder, without even a side-glance.

Such nonchalance was not achieved easily. The hot-house atmosphere of a gaol kept alive resentments which would be carefully stored and paid off at a later opportunity. A 'mix' would be arranged in order to land one's enemy in trouble. These 'mixes' were common between prisoners or between prisoners and warders, and often involved the connivance of a bribed or sympathetic warder. Phelan, popular and tobacco-rich, was able to have a troublesome young warder 'mixed to a standstill'. Friends

spoiled two uniforms with wet cement, dropped fag ends near him when a superior was approaching, hid a light-bulb and a water-tap in his overcoat, 'lost' notes to other convicts telling them he was bribable, praised him as 'one of the best' in the hearing of Principal Warders.

This sort of thing helped convicts to keep their self-respect, to prove to themselves that they were not utterly powerless, and in this emotional jungle nobody was immune. A few months later Phelan incurred the emnity of a fellow convict and became the victim of a series of mixes which lost him all his power and privileges.

Fear of dying in prison haunted all long-term convicts. Macartney suffered bad attacks of anxiety about this during his eight years in Parkhurst and complained:

Deaths in prison are woeful affairs. There is something unutterably lonesome and sad about the idea of dying in a gaol. A convict dies without

friends or relations near him, and is packed in a cheap coffin. The only mourner to walk behind the hearse is the gaoler in charge of searching.

Middle-class, middle-aged star prisoners like Horatio Bottomley and Gerard Lee Bevan, inside for financial chicanery, were allowed to use the hospital as a safe haven. Less privileged prisoners had to resort to devious methods in order to get a few days in hospital. Irritants would be rubbed into the skin to create rashes, soap eaten to make the heart beat erratically and objects swallowed which would necessitate an operation to remove them. One Parkhurst prisoner swallowed a bunch of keys by slipping them off the ring one by one and swallowing them, and another had a lavatory chain, a spoon, several large nails, eight bed springs and part of an aluminium dinner tin removed from his stomach. Stuart Wood, a petty criminal imprisoned for 'telling the tale' (false pretences), tried to give himself blood poisoning from the twine used to sew coal sacks:

With teeth gritted and sweat pouring down my face, I forced that needle through the fleshy parts of my knee, leg and foot so that at least an inch or more of solid flesh was pierced and then drew the thread through the wounds, cutting it off so that it remained in them.

After this painful operation he was allowed three days in bed, but once he recovered he was brought before the governor, charged with malingering and sentenced to more 'strawberries and cream' in the punishment cells.

Lifers and those serving ten-year sentences were aware that confrontation could lead to madness and death. Phelan, coming up for his twelve-year case review – a crucial date for a lifer who hoped to be released with his mental capacities intact – felt himself trapped between Scylla and Charybdis, between apathetic contentment, a condition from which he could easily lapse into delusion and psychosis, and belligerence and resentment, which could only lead to confinement in the punishment cells and an indefinitely delayed release date. The strategy he adopted was one of agonizingly painstaking carefulness: 'I handled my life at that time as a large-size chess game, never neglecting the most insignificant pawn, making no move without considering everything.'

Phelan was released after thirteen and a half years and went on to become a writer and broadcaster. Others were less lucky. Harry Lesbini, who served seventeen years of a life sentence without once infringing the regulations, was released into the uninviting environment of an asylum for the insane. Several other long-term convicts cracked under the strain and, after repeated visits to the punishment cells, found themselves consigned to the Parkhurst 'observation landing'. Here men considered mentally unstable lived their lives in a grim and hopeless limbo:

There seemed something in the psychical atmosphere of the place which hung about it like a pall, creating an indescribable feeling of sorrow and despair. All that was most sad, all that makes life appear darkest and most drear, was there, weighing down the spirits with a sense of grief and loss unutterable ... Several of the inmates had fits, and would fall down while in the exercise yard – the most dreary and depressing spot imaginable, surrounded by high brick walls. Others were simply wrecks of humanity, the dull pallor of whose faces and apathetic look betokened the absence of mind within.

Those 'under observation' were cut off from the normal life of the gaol and once on the 'barmy landing' it was difficult to get off.

Work and play

From the start, convict prisons were organized around the idea of work gangs rather than cell tasks. On arrival each prisoner would be attached to a gang, the choice of which would seriously affect the quality of his life in prison. At Maidstone all the gangs worked within the prison but some enjoyed considerably more freedom than others. 'Trusties' and other favoured prisoners tended to grab the jobs where supervision was minimal, such as those in the library and the gardens. The kitchens were hot and steamy and involved a certain amount of hard work, but they also offered the opportunity to steal food – useful not only to make up the meagre prison rations but to barter for tobacco and other useful commodities and services.

In Parkhurst and Dartmoor the outdoor gangs working in the forests and farms were the most favoured, though there was less enthusiasm for the Dartmoor granite quarries. However, only convicts who had served several years of their sentence and were considered trustworthy were allowed outside the prison walls. Phelan was warned at Dartmoor that the kitchen and the stone-yard, where lumps of granite were pounded into rubble for

Prisoners present themselves for gardening duty at Dartmoor.

road-building, were 'bleedn murder', and the tailor's shop, a stinking crowded loft where the bad-conduct men worked, was even worse:

They did not operate sewing-machines to turn out smart suits of clothes. Instead they sat side by side in rows, to patch and stitch filthy, smelly convict clothes, cast away by the men of the bogs and farms and stables, and instead of the clean, sweet air of the moor, they breathed a compound of granite dust, charcoal fumes and stinking fluff.

Phelan was able to play the prison game cleverly and the old warder in charge of the blacksmith's forge was overjoyed to find someone with a real knowledge and interest in working with metal.

At Parkhurst Phelan wangled his way into an easy job as a gardener, but after being 'mixed' into the punishment cells he was thrust into one of the prison's least favoured work parties, the boot shop. Here he joined men who had tried to escape, men on special watch, men kept in (i.e. confined within the inner wall) for misbehaviour and men considered dangerous subversives, like Wilfred Macartney and the Irish nationalist Frank Breen. Macartney confessed that, despite having spent three and a half years there, he was 'the worst boot-maker who ever hammered a sole', but he was a good lip-still conversationalist and, notwithstanding radical divergence in their political views, he and Phelan gave each other useful backing in their struggles with authority. After Captain Clayton took over in 1930, they staged a 'gaol fight' which resulted in them both being transferred to other, more salubrious, work gangs.

Until 1937 most prison work was unpaid. Only when a prisoner reached Special Stage was he entitled to draw a wage of two shillings and sixpence a week (rising to a maximum of five shillings after a further five years). The tiny minority of prisoners who didn't smoke spent their money on little luxuries like jam, soap, razor blades and tea. Most convicts simply bought tobacco. 'Pigtail', a thin black rope of tobacco, was the standard currency of the prison. According to Phelan:

For an inch of snout a convict could get a clean shirt from a laundryman, a beef dinner from a cook, a couple of decent books from the librarian, a pair of shoes from the boot-maker. For three inches he could hire a bodyguard (a tough to do his fighting for him), or he could buy a decent job from a tobacco-less job holder, or purchase love of a kind among the willowy young effeminates who undulated in every working party.

But the smoking needs of the Special Stage prisoners themselves left too little tobacco to create a proper market. Paradoxically it was the 1937 Home Office order that all prisoners be paid for work and allowed to smoke that caused large-scale trafficking and the emergence of powerful tobacco barons.

As work was generally measured by piece rates, only a handful of unusually diligent or skilful prisoners earned more than a shilling a week. Most convicts invested their pitifully small wages in tobacco, and once their supply ran out they were tempted to borrow from one of the barons, who purchased tobacco from outside via a bent screw. Having borrowed one week – at exorbitant interest rates – it would be difficult not to do the same the next, and before long the victim would be hopelessly entangled. Eventually the baron would, if only to set an example to others,

have the unfortunate debtor beaten up. Frightened men sometimes deliberately had themselves sent to the punishment cells or wriggled their way into hospital, but when they came out the baron's men would be waiting for them. The only effective way to clear the debt was to 'have it away'. It was a prison rule which even barons acknowledged that an escapee should have his debts cancelled. Few of them got very far, and they paid heavily in loss of remission, but this seemed to be a price worth paying for a 'fresh start'.

Tobacco barons tended to be hardened, astute criminals, but they were not immune to danger. Criminal raconteur Charles Raven cites the case of Charlie Marshall, an experienced crook who went into prison with a five-pound note carefully concealed about his person. He invested it in tobacco via a warder and then proceeded to deal very successfully. At the height of his power, however, he upset a warder, who contrived to have him stripped of his accumulated privileges and sent off to the punishment cells. When he returned he found that his henchmen had stolen his tobacco stores, and before long he was in the position of his ex-clients, in debt to the new barons and in constant fear of a beating up.

Wilfred Macartney claimed: 'Tobacco to most of the inhabitants of an industrial state, is almost as much an essential part of their existence as oxygen.' This might seem a bit extreme, even for the nicotine-stained 1930s, but in gaol there were so few pleasures that the narcotic effect of tobacco was highly prized. Certainly there was little pleasure to be gained from prison food. In the twenties experiments were made in giving prisoners a more interesting diet, though in Holloway they were obviously unsuccessful. Kate Meyrick described the dietary regime she found there with fascinated disgust: Sunday's dinner was a small portion of bully beef, a couple of potatoes and a thin slice of bread; Monday's a couple of ounces of rancid bacon; Tuesday's a bowl of pea broth; Wednesday's 'a slab of heavy dough' which was supposed to be suet pudding; Thursday's stewed beef, 'stringy, tough stuff that no human teeth could masticate'; Friday was pea broth again; and on Saturday 'that ghastly suet pudding' once more. Macartney in Parkhurst was equally unimpressed by menus boasting 'treacle pudding', 'savoury bacon', 'beef-steak pudding', 'sea pie,' 'beef stew', 'pork soup', etc.

The vile concoctions masquerading under these honest names might make a hungry pig vomit with disgust. 'Sea pie' is a mess in a filthy tin, defying analysis. The top is a livid scum, patterned with a pallid tracery of cooling grey grease, and just below this fearsome surface rests a lump of grey matter like an incised tumour, the dirty dices of pale pink, half-cooked carrots heightening the diseased anatomical resemblance. The stuff looks as if its real home were a white pail in an operating theatre.

Macartney claimed bitterly: 'One becomes in prison broken-winded, round-shouldered, pot-bellied, and spindle-shanked, and this is really what the system in its hatred of the convict demands, for fear that if the man be decently fed he will rebel.' But it was less a conspiracy by the authorities to underfeed

the inmates of prisons, and more that cheating contractors, trafficking warders, thieving kitchen staffs and bad cooking combined to make prison diet unnutritious and unappetizing. Things were made even worse by the state of the old Victorian prison kitchens: 'Rats, mice and cockroaches abound in them, depositing their droppings in the porridge, consuming the stores and dying in the vats.' The food thus befouled was cooked in out-of-date steamers which reduced it to a dull, unpalatable mass.

Attempts to improve the quality of prison food, however unsuccessful, were meant to benefit the physical welfare of prisoners. Efforts were also made to improve their mental and moral welfare: evening classes, prison visitors, concerts and even film shows were arranged. In a poorly run prison these sorts of activities were grudgingly undertaken and cynically received, but a good governor like Clayton was able to take advantage of the climate of liberalization to improve the lives of his charges. At Parkhurst the band of intelligent, articulate prisoners led by Phelan, Macartney and the leaders of the Dartmoor Mutiny (who were dumped on Clayton as the only man likely to be able to handle such intractable characters) were allowed to start a prison news-sheet, and form a jazz band and a chess club. But the great amount of time that convicts spent alone in their cells meant their main intellectual efforts went into reading.

Macartney's chapters on prison reading reveal an acute literary sensibility among the Parkhurst convicts – their enjoyment of Evelyn Waugh, their contempt for Edgar Wallace, their high regard for Patrick Hamilton, their impatience with Galsworthy. Prisoners were allowed two novels and two non-fiction books a fortnight in First Stage and more as they progressed through the stages. But getting hold of the books one wanted was a risky business and depended on the whims and fancies of the gaolers and 'trusties' who worked in the library. Macartney used to bribe the librarians with tobacco. 'It was just business: no books, no 'bacca.'

Swapping books with other prisoners was widespread but it was punishable by three days' bread and water in the punishment cells and loss of remission and privileges. Macartney, who was an inveterate lender of books, had one narrow escape when a prisoner he had lent a book to died, and a second when another was sent to the punishment cells for assaulting a warder. He was finally caught out when his bound volume of *Labour Monthly* was found in the cell of a prisoner who had tried to escape. After this he made potential borrowers answer the following three questions before he would lend out a book:

1   Are you going to 'chin' a screw while you have my book in your possession?
2   Are you going to attempt to escape?
3   Are you going to die on me?

Convicts with money were able to buy in books from outside, as long as the authorities deemed them to be suitable reading, and Macartney's constant haranguing resulted in him building up an impressive collection of Marxist books. His great moment of triumph came when he discovered that the Standing Orders decreed that the number of books a Special Stage prisoner was allowed in his cell depended on the discretion of the chaplain. By browbeating the chaplain he managed to get all the books he had acquired in his eight years at Parkhurst brought to his cell:

That evening I spent a joyous couple of hours arranging Marx's *Capital*, three volumes, and his *Gotha Programme*, and *Civil War in France*; Lenin, five volumes: Stalin, two volumes; Engels, four volumes: Bukharin, Palme Dutt, Allan Hutt, Pollitt etc., and about three volumes of bound periodicals. They looked swell on my three shelves, tightly and tidily packed – the only tidy thing in the room.

But this proved to be a short-lived victory. Governor Clayton left shortly afterwards and the new regime soon found excuses to remove Macartney's books.

The prison autobiographies are full of touching stories about the relationships of lonely convicts with birds, cats, mice, rats and dogs, but the main preoccupation of the vast majority of prisoners was with sex. According to Jim Phelan: 'Sex claimed everything – thought, vocabulary, fantasy, memory and action. Drooping, bent-spined, hollow-cheeked "Lifers" clawed avidly for books that might hold a stimulating picture.' Phelan managed to have an illicit relationship with an IRA-supporting governor's governess at Parkhurst. He had a peasant suspicion of homosexuality, but others were more ready to make use of substitutes. Macartney thought fondly on his wife, who stood by him and visited him regularly during the eight years he spent inside, but after four years he found his dreams suffused with homosexual imagery:

Even when awake I began to find that fantastic images were pushing the original normal image out of the way. Gradually a homosexual shadow obscured the normal picture, and I began to have definitely homosexual dreams. I do not propose to enlarge further upon my own sex life, but I shall assert that within my observation the beneficial effects of such contacts upon the mental and physical health were undeniable, and my experience was that of the average man. Of course some repressed themselves terribly and never consciously entered into this life. Others went to extremes and developed perversions that would make Krafft-Ebing's hair stand upright.

Prisoners who were unabashed about being effeminately homosexual – most of whom were in prison for non-sexual offences – tended to do well in prison. With their rouged faces (from the dye in mailbags) and margarined kiss curls they had little difficulty attracting admirers and protectors. Macartney regarded them as 'among the coolest, and frequently the soundest, men in the prison'. Nora and Elsie ('a tall, well-built blond, always beautifully made-up, with trim golden hair, plucked and pencilled eyebrows, schoolgirl complexion, and rouged lips') enjoyed considerable prestige at Parkhurst. Nora's love affair with a prison officer allowed him to enhance his charms with scent, ribbons and silk underwear. He and his warder lover were lucky in having the whole landing collude in their love affair. But this was exceptional and generally a desperate ingenuity was called for. Fortunately convicts were experts at 'taking the dairy' (distracting attention at crucial moments) and Eric Parr, a thirties 'peterman' (safe-breaker), reports

that a couple even managed to consummate their passion while queuing outside the governor's office. Homosexual relations could cause jealousy and friction which would sometimes erupt into two men fighting over their shared beloved. But they generally reduced tension and helped in the harmonious running of the gaol.

Phelan makes the interesting claim that most of the sex cases at Parkhurst were guilt-ridden suppressed homosexuals and that ironically – in view of the authorities' complete inability to offer any sort of treatment which might prevent them continuing in dangerously sadistic practices – a surprising number of them were cured of their sadism, bestiality and paedophilia by a fulfilling prison romance.

The hundred varieties of sadism for which a large percentage of convicts are gaoled are only man-centred sex-urges unrecognized. People chop off babies' legs, excrete in churches or offices, skin mice, lash little girls, burn cats, use knives in unmentionable ways on little boys, slash women with razors, use red-hot pokers, rape six-month babies, stick skewers in living rabbits, hack, chop, stab, slash, scald and bludgeon their relatives or lovers, run through all the gibbering fantastic bedlam gamut of pain-making, then find their way to Maidstone or Parkhurst or Dartmoor.

There, if they chose to mix with the Lilys and Veras, the Dollys and Noras, 'they were cured of their fantastic preconceptions and weird unmentionable practices'. Phelan's argument might now seem over-optimistic but it is seductively attractive in an otherwise gloomy area of prison life.

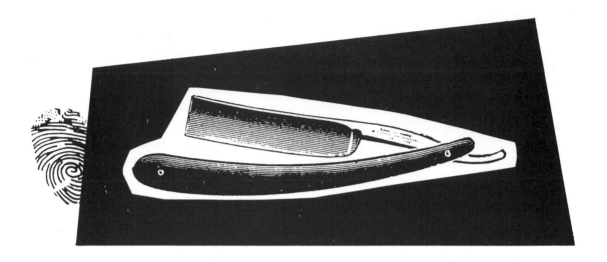

6 DESPERATE MEASURES

Inside the gate everything changes with a painful swiftness. The freshness and freedom, the clean open bigness of the Moor, are expunged in a second, giving way to narrow fetid passage and towering wall, to the thwartings of a myriad minor barriers and blockades, to an incredible cramping of outlook, to restriction and stifling and stink.

Jim Phelan, Jail Journey (1940)

Mutiny

Mutiny was difficult to organize in an English prison: gaol society was riddled with informers and it was impossible to keep anything involving more than two or three men secret. The mutiny that occurred at Dartmoor on the morning of 24 January 1932 was an outbreak of rage and frustration of which the authorities had had plenty of warning. It succeeded because they couldn't imagine it would actually happen. As Macartney comments sarcastically, 'In the minds of the authority, the idea that mutinous convicts could seize a prison seemed impossible – like horses talking or sheep singing. When the horses did talk and the sheep began singing, so amazed were the gaolers that they just panicked, and flew for their lives to the gate.'

Compared with the 1990 Strangeways riot, the Dartmoor Mutiny, when for a few brief hours prisoners threw off their shackles and took control of the gaol, seems a mild enough affair, but it brought the secretive English prison system on to the front page and came to assume a symbolic importance out of all proportion to the tiny threat it offered.

There had been earlier intimations that a prison could erupt into mutiny. The politically motivated Sinn Fein prisoners at Portland were considered a danger in 1921 but a combination of tactical concessions and dispersal to other prisons defused the threat. Parkhurst had come close to a spontaneous mutiny during the last days of Colonel Hales. His stubborn attempt to stop convicts talking after the 'no talking' rule had been abolished provoked a rebellious spirit in the prison

which only subsided with the arrival of Captain Clayton. But Parkhurst was, in relative terms, a pleasant prison; in Dartmoor's granite halls the mists, the isolation and the constant dampness were an additional aggravation to convicts serving long sentences under a harsh regime. Val Davis, who served part of his ten-year sentence at Dartmoor, complained that a hundred years of viciousness, evil and mistrust between captive and gaoler had left 'a malignant root in the foundations of the present prison':

It is Dartmoor's 'legacy of hate', bequeathed by those criminals who died under its iron rule in years gone by. It is no phantom of the imagination, but a real thing. Every warder and convict to-day is aware that a barrier exists that prevents willing co-operation. This vicious influence holds undisputed sway, the worst type of prisoner reacts to it with little provocation. The present staff officers have partly shelved the 'big stick' of former dispensations – but it is beyond them to heal the mental wounds it has left.

Davis thought that the seeds of the mutiny were sown back in 1924, when four popular prisoners made an escape bid and were brutally beaten on their recapture. A succession of fair and reasonable governors between 1925 and 1931 – Captain Morgan, Captain Clayton, Major Morris – kept the lid on discontent, but it rose to the boil during the insensitive regime of Governor Roberts.

Morgan, Clayton and Morris had – as far as it was possible within Dartmoor's dank and dangerous walls – tried to foster a spirit of harmony and co-operation. Clayton had allowed the convicts extra privileges such as coconut matting for the damp floors of their cells, prison visitors from Toc H, the working man's charity, instead of the well-meaning but ineffectual gentlemen of leisure who normally fulfilled this function, and evening classes on a variety of subjects. The new governor, A. N. Roberts, was encouraged by reactionary elements in the Prison Commission to put an end to the spirit of 'laxness' that was thought to have permeated Britain's most feared prison. Ruby Sparks, who had been rearrested in 1931 and was serving a long sentence in Dartmoor, described the Governor as 'a tall, bloated man with a black Stalin moustache and beefy-red face' who dressed in a tweed jacket and riding breeches. But Roberts was exceptional in having experienced life as an ordinary prison warder and was nothing like the empty-headed ex-army and navy officers who infested the prison service. However, he seems to have gone about his task in the worst possible way. Lags were virtually forced into attending chapel by being denied concerts and news-readings if they didn't; evening classes, which depended on the good-will of unpaid volunteers, were discouraged; it was made even more difficult than before to transfer from one work party to another; and warders were urged to report the slightest infringement of discipline.

Prisoners' grievances came to a head on the weekend of 23/24 January. There had been complaints for several weeks that the food was even worse than usual and on some mornings the porridge was inedible. On Saturday 23 January, after a week of unrest, Roberts tried to address the convicts assembled at chapel. He was shouted down and a

riot might have broken out there and then but for the persistence of the chaplain in proceeding with the hymn-singing. Reprisals followed and several men were taken from their cells and dragged off to the punishment block. The authorities were alarmed by the continuing unrest and Colonel Turner, an Assistant Prison Commissioner, arrived that night to take charge of the gaol. By this time, however, things had got out of hand. The following morning convicts were incensed by the sobs and shrieks of 'Silly Arthur', a weak-minded prisoner being bludgeoned by the warders for his 'innzlence'. When they were let out into the exercise yards they refused to obey orders and the mutiny began.

Roberts was convinced (rightly) that the convicts were determined to do him serious injury and beat a rapid retreat. Colonel Turner – the only prison official who didn't flee – was jostled, had his watch dropped down a drain and a bowl of porridge poured over his head when he tried to remonstrate with the rioters. But on the whole, the convicts behaved with good humour and restraint and no warder was seriously injured. Having gained control of the interior of the prison, the mutineers contented themselves with releasing men held in the punishment block, rifling and burning down the administrative block where their records were kept, and raiding the warders' quarters for beer and tobacco. Sparks recalled that the atmosphere was almost festive, with jubilant convicts singing and dancing and playing tunelessly but enthusiastically on purloined band instruments:

Dartmoor burning during the 1932 mutiny.

Beer barrels from the warders' canteen had been dragged out into the yard. Handfuls of cigarettes were being passed around, and several comical old lags had two or three lit cigarettes in their mouths at once. Dozens of them had got drunk on their first swig of beer after being locked away all those years, and were staggering around in each other's arms singing 'Sweet Adeline'.

But the fun lasted only a few hours. By lunchtime a detachment of Plymouth police had recaptured the prison and by the early hours of the afternoon all the prisoners were either back in their cells or in hospital.

The police acted with admirable modera-tion but once the warders regained control of the prison savage beatings followed. Dr Guy Richmond, one of the prison doctors, reck-oned that he and his colleagues 'must have sutured the scalps of at least seventy victims'. The Home Office commissioned Herbert du Parcq, a barrister, to investigate and write a report on the mutiny. Du Parcq carried out his task very efficiently – appointed on 25 January, he arrived at Dartmoor on the 26th, spent three days interviewing officers and convicts, and wrote up his report by 3 Febru-ary. Unfortunately du Parcq's speed was not matched by his perspicacity and he seemed extraordinarily shy of making any sort of criticism of the Prison Service.

Du Parcq constructs an Alice in Wonderland world where responsibility for the unsettled state of the prison lay not with the authorities but with four (unnamed) ringleaders 'of the motor bandit type'; where, despite the fact that on consecutive days the food was so bad that the Governor had to order special rations of bully beef and potatoes, 'there was no reasonable grounds for complaint of the food'; where the output of work parties was increasing but a reduction in staffing levels had cut the convicts' working day to less than five and a half hours. Thus he was able to reach the conclusion that 'the prisoners had no substantial grievances and that such grievances as they had would not have led to any disorder unless a few of the dangerous prisoners, partly by their power of leadership, partly by intimidation, had played on the feelings and fears of others.'

Du Parcq's stress on the resourcefulness of the new type of 'motor bandit' criminal finds an echo in Macartney's description of Ruby Sparks:

Ruby was one of the most reliable men it has been my fortune to meet, shrewd, able, and energetic. He is a type that our present society seems unable to use to the advantage of society as a whole. It turns people like Ruby Sparks into motor bandits, and makes paranoiacs like Hitler and Goering the arbiters of the destinies of millions.

The same qualities could be found in legendary bandits like Jack Sheppard or Robin Hood. To put the blame on such men for stirring up their docile but stupid fellow convicts was absurd, but that is what the authorities proceeded to do.

A number of ringleaders were selected and brought to trial at an improvised courtroom in Princetown in April 1932. Two men were charged with wounding with intent to commit grievous bodily harm, thirty with riotous conduct and wilful damage. Several of the charges were dismissed, but the sentences on those found guilty showed that the authorities had no intention of admitting responsibility or of treating leniently men driven to desperate acts. Between them the mutineers received sentences of almost a hundred years. One of them, 'Beaver' Ibbetson, who had only six months left of his three-year sentence to serve, received another ten years and within months had collapsed into insanity. Another, Billy Mitchell, who had been shot through the throat 'while attempting to escape' (his real offence had been shouting abuse from the rooftops), was permanently paralysed but was still made to serve out his sentence, much of it in the punishment cells.

Ruby Sparks received an additional sentence of four years. But he had not spent all his time in Dartmoor eating tables in the punishment block, and a newly acquired knowledge of the workings of the law helped him uncover a blunder made by the authorities. His original ten-year sentence consisted of five years' penal servitude and five years' preventive detention. Sparks successfully appealed that preventive detention – a form of sentence designed to deal with the hardened criminal by putting him away for a long period but giving him extra privileges which would encourage the process of reform – could only be served directly after the penal servitude it was linked to. By interposing an additional four years, his five years' preventive detention was now null and void. By June 1938 he was out, but within a few months he was caught house-breaking and returned to Dartmoor to serve another four-year sentence.

Escapes

Mutiny was an exceptional response to the awfulness of prison life. The more usual choices were stoicism, resignation, madness or the dreadful schizophrenic existence of the grass. The other alternative was to escape.

Attempted escapes from English gaols were common, successful escapes much rarer. Phelan makes the point that few prisoners had the resources of patience and endurance to plan their escape properly, and that most escapers were merely 'taking a chance', making a desperate bid for freedom which was almost certain to fail. Of the three convict stations, Maidstone was the easiest to escape from, but the predominance of 'star' prisoners meant that one was unlikely to find the sort of advice and support one might expect from the recidivists of Dartmoor and Parkhurst. Dartmoor presented special problems because of its siting. The prison stood on the edges of the 'Great' and 'Little' Mires and crossing the treacherous peat bogs without a guide was extremely hazardous. If a convict did get away there was no wild chase because warders could rely on the Moor to deliver their quarry. Phelan points out that

after the first few minutes every warder goes to his previously appointed place, first on an inner circle, then on an outer. He stays there. Small parties call at various known hiding holes. Sooner or later the Mug will crawl up to the gun, because every exit from the Moor is known and posted. There is very little of the dramatic about it. Hunger and cold and dampness make the man change his cherished plan every time. He tries to get off the Moor in the quiet of the night. Even if he does not wander back to the gaol, even if he has been told of the ways to take, the screw is waiting for him at the end. There is no need to chase a fugitive through a maze, if one knows the exits and has plenty of time to spare.

Parkhurst was not a particularly easy prison to break out of, particularly after the building of the outer wall in the late twenties, but stories abound of men escaping from the prison only to fail in their attempts to get off the island. Even during the holiday season it was not easy for an escaped convict to evade detection by the suspicious and unsympathetic islanders. Macartney complained bitterly that 'when a man escapes on the Isle of Wight the whole population, from Royal Yacht Squadron to retired Pompey whores, turns out to catch him', and tells a tale of a man who found shelter in the bed of a farmer's widow and remained with her for fifteen years, only to be shopped to the authorities when 'she had no further use for him in the bed or the field'.

An escape was an important event in the cultural life of the prison. Even a hopeless escape could be seen as a brave act of defiance and uplifted the spirits of the prisoners and caused grim consternation among the gaolers. Despite the fact that while an escape alert was on all privileges were suspended and convicts spent most of their time locked in their cells, captured escapees were treated as heroes by their fellow prisoners – but they were treated harshly by their captors. Even if they avoided being beaten, they lost remission and privileges and were sent to the punishment cells for their 'Welcome Home' party – fifteen days' bread and water, forty-two days' porridge and potatoes. When they emerged it was to a new and harsher regime. They had to wear clothes sewn with big coloured patches to make them more conspicuous, they were kept on inside working parties and closely supervised, and they had to leave their clothes outside their cell and sleep with the light on at night.

Fortunately, determined escapers tended to be extremely resilient, using their escape plans and their war with the authorities as a means of preserving their integrity and self-respect. Unjustly imprisoned burglar Alfie Hinds was lodged in Chelmsford, one of the newly designated preventive detention prisons in 1958, and fought back vigorously against regulations unchanged since the twenties. Annoyed at warders kicking on his door 'to make sure it was him and not a dummy in the bed', he decided to beat them at their own game:

The next night, I deliberately faced my bed away towards the window and kept perfectly still under the blankets. When the night-watchman kicked on the door, I didn't budge an inch. He kicked again, he kicked a third time, even louder. I had arranged with the other prisoners on the landing to take this as the signal to break into an uproar, embarrassing to the authorities because there were a number of private houses near the prison. Everyone started shouting and banging. I kept motionless. About a quarter of an hour later, there was a sound of tramping along the corridor. A posse of warders halted outside my cell and the door was flung open. I looked up sleepily. 'What on earth's the matter?' I said. 'What's all the noise about?'

A few weeks later Hinds escaped.

Most escapes failed, so when Ruby Sparks broke out of Dartmoor and remained free for five months it was an extraordinary achievement. Sparks had already escaped from Strangeways in 1927 when he sawed through his cell bars and climbed over the wall at four in the morning in a suit made out of his blankets. Unfortunately he missed his connection with the 'Bobbed-Haired Bandit' and was caught a day or two later, wet and dishevelled, making for Liverpool.

His escape from Dartmoor on 10 January 1940 was more carefully planned. Since his arrival there in February 1939 Sparks and two collaborators, Dick Nolan and Alec Marsh, had been working on the rope and five master keys they would need to get out. They managed to keep their plans secret, and successfully to break out of the prison. Nolan and Sparks separated from Marsh and made their way along the railway line to Plymouth, where, exhausted, they fell asleep in a freight wagon. When they awoke it was daylight and they were trundling into Devonport Naval Dockyard. Their luck held, though, and, after various adventurous bus and train journeys, they eventually reached London, where they had helpful friends in the underworld.

Alec Marsh remained free for six days, Dick Nolan for four months. Sparks succeeded in holding out until 28 June, mainly because of the help and support he had from the 'Bobbed-Haired Bandit', but it was a disillusioning experience for both of them:

I was a bit taken aback how shocked her face was. I'd tried to spruce up before I saw her, and had got a lot of the muck off, but my fingers and mouth were burst open with frostbite and from so much punishment diet. I'd got sores all over me like sailors used to get before they found out about lime juice. She looked at me and I looked at her. The King and Queen of smash and grab. She looked older and tired and there was grey in her hair and the beginnings of lines down the side of her mouth. I saw that she was screwing up her eyes to see me, and I asked her, 'Lil, do you wear spectacles now?' She looked a bit uncomfortable and said, 'Yes, sometimes, but only for reading.'

Billy Hill recruited Sparks for a series of smash and grab raids, but in April he was caught after an abortive robbery in Bond Street. Sparks discovered that few other underworld figures were prepared to work with someone so hotly pursued by Scotland Yard. He tired of being cooped up in Lilian Goldstein's Wembley Park home. The glamour of their earlier life together had drained away completely and they got on each other's nerves. To relieve the boredom Sparks set up a robbery with two young tearaways, but their violent tendencies disturbed him and sickened Goldstein. It was almost a relief when the police – in the form of Peter Beveridge, Edward Greeno and Robert Higgins – recaptured him and returned him to Dartmoor.

Lilian Goldstein was convicted of harbouring a gaol-breaker and sentenced to six months' imprisonment. But Sir Gerald Dodson, the Recorder of London, cancelled the sentence, commenting that he'd given a great deal of thought to the case and come to the conclusion that 'in doing what you did, although it was breaking the law, you followed a natural womanly instinct in trying to succour and protect this man, with whom you had intimate relations over a period of years'. Characteristically, the 'Bobbed-Haired Bandit' shed no tears of gratitude and made no comment as she left the dock.

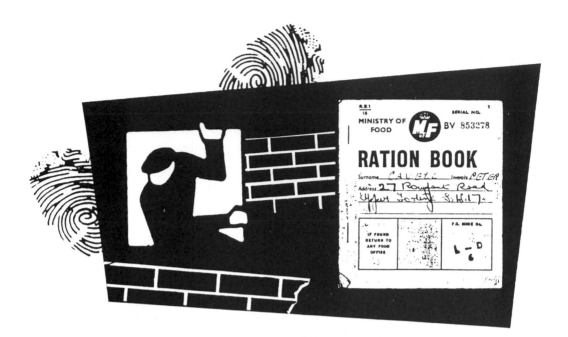

7 THE UNDERWORLD AT WAR

Up in his room with the door locked he was going over all the things he'd be needing. They were spread out on the bed in front of him. There was his knuckleduster – the hedgehog. And a pair of kid gloves that wouldn't leave fingerprints. And a screwdriver. And a pair of dark glasses that might come in handy. And his cosh. Last of all there was his bunch of car keys. 'Only fools carry a gun,' he said to console himself for not having one.

Norman Collins, *London Belongs to Me* (1945)

Wartime crime

The war affected the underworld as much as it did everyone else. Attempts to ignore it and carry on as normal proved futile. Those who threw away their call-up papers found themselves pursued by military police – rougher and less amenable to bribery than their civilian counterparts – and drafted into the army. Italians, as undesirable aliens, fared particularly badly, and gangsters who for years had thought themselves invulnerable found themselves interned alongside ice-cream salesmen and film producers. However, the depleted ranks of the professional criminals were soon filled by enthusiastic amateurs, eager to take advantage of the favourable new conditions provided by the war.

The twenties and thirties were far from the crime-free golden age they sometimes appear in retrospect, but the police remained firmly in control and were treated with a certain amount of deference. The war shifted the balance of power in favour of the criminals. The pre-war underworld had been concerned either with semi-legal activities (gambling, drugs and prostitution) or with robbing the rich. It was not until the war years, with the growth of commodity crime and the black market, that the underworld became parasitic on the community at large.

One might have expected that, with the country in danger of invasion, differences would be forgotten in the common struggle and crime would diminish. Billy Hill, who was released from Chelmsford when war broke out, was prepared to admit that, 'In some respects we were a common herd in those days, with a common enemy.' But, like most criminals, his altruistic intentions were soon eroded by the new opportunities for crime that the war opened up. He managed to avoid military service and take advantage of wartime disruption to expand his activities. Like many other crooks, he had never had it so good:

Money? It was coming to us like pieces of dirty paper. I rarely went out with less than a monkey or a grand in my pocket. That was spending stuff. Emergency funds in case I got nicked, or in case the bite was put on me. That was apart from the remainder of a steady fortune I had piling up.

Stylish nonchalance: a late forties spiv.

As a relief from the problems of smash and grab raids – getaway driving, interfering passers-by, untrustworthy buyers – he sought an alternative source of income. Rejecting banks as too cluttered up with anti-burglar devices, he began a successful series of attacks on the post offices of Greater London. The blackout and a depleted police force meant that, having broken in, Hill and his gang could generally work undisturbed on the safe with their specially made safe-rippers. A working hole was drilled in the side of the safe and Hill's giant tin-opener was inserted to cut it open 'just like opening a corned-beef tin'. Hill reckoned on an average haul of around £3,000 a week from these post office robberies, but he was unable to resist a good smash and grab raid and was inspired to launch a new campaign by the escape of Ruby Sparks from Dartmoor in January 1940. Sparks welcomed the opportunity of working with Hill, but after a couple of escapades together Hill was caught when his getaway car mounted the pavement and entangled its bumpers in the railings, and he was sentenced to another two years in Chelmsford gaol.

Criminals drafted into the services were often alienated and frustrated by the petty tyranny of army life. Jack Spot, the Jewish East End gangster, found as much anti-semitism in the army as he had outside, and made so much trouble for the authorities that he was eventually given a medical discharge. Home Secretary Herbert Morrison intervened in the fate of Ruby Sparks after visiting him in the punishment cells at Dartmoor and gave him the chance to put his resourcefulness and ingenuity to good use in the army. Sparks 'had an idea it would be like the companionship of a good thieving team in the old days, the risks and jokes, the careful planning of a job, then going in there with your heart pounding', but he came up against a swaggering bully of a corporal who misguidedly tried to make the ex-burglar's life a misery. Not surprisingly, this led to violent confrontations. Within weeks Sparks had deserted and resumed his criminal career.

More adaptable criminals with less public reputations found plenty of opportunities to employ their talents in the services; particularly in supplying the black market. War made even the most mundane commodities – from bacon to gardening tools, from stockings to safety pins – valuable and thus significantly expanded the market for stolen goods. Rationing, which prevented those who had money from buying as much as they wished, meant there was a steady supply of eager customers for black-market goods. The blackout and the shortage of policemen – the youngest and fittest of them had been drafted into the army – meant that goods stored in warehouses, railway depots, docks and factories were vulnerable to determined bands of thieves.

Officially the black market operated on a minor and unimportant level during the war. According to Lord Woolton, the Minister of Food:

The penalties for infringement of the food regulations were literally ruinous ... and the consequence was that [black marketeering] became so perilous an occupation that few indeed dared embark on it . . . in spite of all scarcity of supplies and the rigidity of rationing, there was little or no black market in Britain.

This is completely untrue. Black-market activity was a thorn in the side of the government from the beginning of the war. Though the rationing system never actually broke down, it suffered severe haemorrhages. The market towns around London – Chelmsford, Braintree, Watford, Maidstone and Romford – attracted hordes of London dealers who exchanged their gowns, cloth and manufactured goods for agricultural produce with no regard whatsoever for the rationing system. In 1944, 14,000 ration books were stolen from a government office in Hertfordshire, 600,000 supplementary clothing coupons from a London employment exchange, and 100,000 ration books from the Romford Food Office. The Romford ration books were reckoned to be worth half a million pounds on the black market, making it the most lucrative haul until the Great Train Robbery of 1963; the thieves were never caught and none of the ration books was recovered.

In Romford, the black-market centre of the south-east, cloth, meat and millions of eggs were sold ('for hatching') to wholesalers signing themselves 'Neville Chamberlain' and 'Winston Churchill', and the Upton Park gypsies led by Arthur Skurry grew fat and powerful as self-appointed protectors of these dubious transactions, making sure – for a price – that nothing was spoilt or broken. The undermanned police force could do little to interrupt the smooth flow of business. Large numbers of enthusiastic amateurs took to pilfering from shops, warehouses, factories and docks to feed the growing black market.

Bombing raids left shops and homes open to the elements and looting was more of a problem than the authorities were prepared to admit at the time. Deserters and professional criminals took advantage of the blackout to smash their way into shops and houses – and not always those that were bomb-damaged. After the war, the Chief Constable of Liverpool confessed to the *Police Chronicle and Constabulary World*:

The raids on the city left many premises very easy to break into, and premises made unfit for occupation provided cover from which to attack adjoining premises and also for hiding stolen goods. The shortages of all kinds of food and clothing made it easy for thieves to dispose of stolen property and also made it worthwhile to steal what before the war would not have repaid the trouble and risk. Crimes on a large scale were often instigated by operators in the Black Market, and on many occasions a whole lorry load of goods was stolen . . . Deserters from the Forces and the Mercantile Marine were responsible for many offences and were not easy to catch as their visits were often of very short duration.

By the middle years of the war the underworld had become sufficiently aware of the profits to be made from the black market to organize large-scale depredations in the form of lorry hijacks and warehouse robberies. In one theft alone 1,366,000 cigarettes were stolen.

The rise of the spiv

Mark Benney, by this time well established as a novelist and social commentator, argues

Man of the people: a nondescript spiv selling nylons.

that during the war years a new kind of criminal underworld emerged out of the ruins of the old:

The growth of the 'black market' diverted a large part of the purchasing power of the country through criminal channels; small-time thieves, with long, depressing police-histories, found it had suddenly become ludicrously easy to acquire hundreds of pounds with very little risk. Only the very stupidest could fail to flourish like the green bay tree if he could contrive to evade the Essential Works Order; and the very scale of illicit opportunity has enforced something like commercial organization on the underworld. Traditions have broken down here as elsewhere. Bosses have arisen with organizing experience and capital; affiliations with Paris, Brussels, and New York are no longer thriller-writers' dreams; the supply of young men who are willing to carry a gun for a wide 'head' is ample. Moreover, the distinction between criminal and non-criminal has become most conveniently blurred and the old habits of criminal isolation and segregation are falling rapidly out of use.

The pre-war underworld was almost a separate caste: they spoke a language so riddled with argot and rhyming slang that it was virtually impossible for an outsider to comprehend. The war brought about a dilution of this criminal subculture as large numbers of deserters and petty racketeers swelled the ranks of the underworld, and a new figure moved into the limelight – the spiv.

Nothing so clearly indicates changing attitudes to crime as the rise of the spiv as a popular figure in the public imagination. In its original sense, a spiv was a clearly defined criminal species – a runner or contact man – someone who brought people together for criminal endeavours and took a commission on any business they did together. As such they tended to be unobtrusive, diplomatic sorts of men, capable of spending a lot of time hanging around without drawing attention to themselves. The spiv popularized by Arthur English and Sid Field on the variety circuits, Osbert Lancaster in his *Daily Express* cartoons, Michael Medwin, Griffith Jones and Nigel Patrick on the cinema screen was rather different. With his relentless, persuasive chat, his flashily expensive dress, and his ability to mediate between the underworld and the law-abiding citizenry, he became an icon of the austerity years.

The black market had transformed the links between the public and the criminal world and required a different sort of contact man, a recognizable type who could be approached in the same way that a prostitute was approached – with a certain confidence that illicit requests would not be rejected. Spivs adopted the style of dress of the more fashion-conscious of the racing gangsters of the thirties, a sizeable contingent of whom were Jewish or Italian with friends or relations in the rag trade. In many ways the spivs marked a transition between the criminal underworld, where there was a long tradition of flamboyant dressing, and the rebellious teen culture of the Teddy boys.

David Hughes, in his wrong-headed but irresistible article on 'The Spivs' in *The Age of Austerity*, captures their style beautifully:

Rings flashed on middle fingers, hats were crushed rakishly down on duck-arse haircuts, and the mood, as if sustained from the war, was one of tough casual humour in the face of grave hard-ships: such as how to dispose at high speed of a hot lorryload of socks, twelve and a tanner in the stores, four bob to you. Luckily for the spiv, a surprisingly large number of people were soon wearing the socks (or drinking the Scotch or luxuriating in the sheets), and keeping mum about it.

The wartime black market was much bigger than was officially admitted, but it was a secretive, disreputable affair. When the war ended people expected conditions to improve: an end to shortages and restrictions, the beginning of the good life for which they had fought. The dire economic situation made austerity inevitable but it seemed an unfair price to pay for victory. People grew impatient and thought it unfair that ration-ing and queuing were even worse than before. Respect for law and order dwindled and the colourful, eager to please spiv, 'flash-ily displaying all the suppressed energies of the back streets', seemed a more attractive proposition to deal with than the surly, arro-gant shopkeeper. With everything in short supply, and the new Labour government trying to ensure equitable shares for every-body, the black market boomed.

It is easy to glamorize the black market, to see it as a healthy protest against bureau-cratic strangulation, but there was a very seedy side to it. Arthur Helliwell, a popular columnist on the *People*, declared that Britain had become 'the land of the well-greased palm':

We've developed into a nation of bribers. Everyone is on the game, from the big shot who buys the motor dealer's wife a fur coat and gets delivery of a new car in a week, to the housewife who slips the fishmonger a packet of cigarettes after the queue has gone. The butcher runs a car, but he can't get much petrol – slip him a couple of coupons and get an extra steak for yourself. The coal merchant can't get eggs – send him a couple of dozen and there's a ton of coal in your cellar. A page of clothing coupons to your tobacconist – and there'll always be a packet of twenty under the counter for you.

Except for a small minority of working-class people who participated in its profits, the black market inevitably benefited the rich more than the poor, by subverting a rationing system designed to ensure fair shares for all.

Most spivs were amateur, part-time crimi-nals, men scraping a living on the fringes of the law, but those at the top of the pile were professional criminals like Billy Hill, who, with his expertise as a burglar, his capacity for organization and his ability to attract inside information, soon established a lucra-tive business as a black marketeer. In order to cope with the large quantities of stolen goods coming in, he acquired a rambling eighteenth-century manor house in the sleepy Hertfordshire village of Bovingdon, be-tween Rickmansworth and Berkhamsted:

Our Bovingdon run-in was packed tight with bent gear and I now had a relay of my own cars bringing it up to London as the demand needed it. All I had to do was to take a stroll around the West End and I was literally besieged by people wanting to buy almost anything from a pair of nylon stockings to a fresh salmon or a shoulder of good smoked bacon. There were many times when that barn was filled chock-a-block with nicked gear – sheets, towels, furniture, shoes, textiles, rolls of silk, tea, tobacco, sugar, even rare spices which fetched a fortune from the Soho café proprietors who needed that sort of thing.

Hill seems to have had no trouble with the villagers or the local police, but severe petrol rationing made constant to-ing and fro-ing between London and Bovingdon difficult. He solved the problem by devising a complex racket involving forged petrol coupons which became a lucrative business in itself.

Profits from the black market were high and the risks seemed low. Hill began wearing forty-guinea suits, silk shirts and hand-made shoes and indulging in the conspicuous display characteristic of spivery. On Mondays, the underworld's 'day off', he would join his fellow gangsters in a club in Archer Street. 'What with all the villains in their genuine Savile Row suits and their wives and girl-friends wearing straight furs and clothes by the best West End dressmakers, the club looked like the Ascot of the underworld.'

However, the boom was too good to last, though the danger came less from the under-manned and overworked police force than from internal conflict between gangsters grown reckless and arrogant with all this easy money.

Billy Hill at the Bovingdon run-in.

8 STRUGGLES FOR POWER

Comer is known as Jack Sprott. He is thought – almost certainly – to be the brains behind the London Airport bullion robbery attempt in 1948 and the £250,000 mailvan theft last year. Comer frequents most of the Soho betting clubs and does a lot of pavement edge betting in Gt. Windmill Street, outside Jack Solomons's gym. I think there is a tie-up somewhere between Comer and Solomons. Comer is invariably attended by a bevy of smoothly dressed 'gorillas' and I have seen him in company of a very attractive dark-haired woman.

Memo from Baggott to *Daily Mirror* News Desk, September 1953

The post-war crime boom

While the war was on there was a determined attempt not to let any sign of social breakdown alarm the public and damage morale. Once the external enemies were defeated, attention focused on internal problems – one of which was the crime boom. The police had not fared well during the war. Between 1940 and 1944 their numbers were reduced by 14,000 as the younger, fitter members of the force were drafted into the services. When the war ended, drastic measures were taken to halt the crime wave. On the night of 14 December 1945, 2,000 policemen invaded Soho and checked the papers of everybody they came across in the pubs, cafés, dance-halls and gambling clubs. A shocked Mark Benney, writing in that second week of December, recorded:

The crime wave for which the police have been preparing ever since the end of hostilities is breaking upon us. Armed robberies of the most violent and vicious kind feature daily in the newspapers. Even the pettiest crimes are, it seems, conducted with a loaded revolver to hand. And well-planned robberies, reminiscent of the heyday of Chicago gangsterdom, have relieved Londoners of £60,000 worth of jewellery in the past week alone. Hold-ups of cinemas, post offices, and railway booking offices have already become so commonplace that the newspapers scarcely bother to report them. To deal with the situation the police are being forced to adopt methods more akin to riot-breaking than crime detection.

Early the following January, checkpoints were set up on all the major roads leading in and out of London, and on all the Thames bridges between Tower Bridge and Hammersmith, in an attempt to round up some of the 20,000 deserters reckoned to be on the loose.

These military-style operations were partly a matter of public relations, to demonstrate how actively crime was being combated and to attract recruits due for demobilization from the services. A more serious threat to the professional criminals was the establishment on 1 January 1946 of the 'Ghost Squad', an undercover unit headed by Chief Superintendent John 'Charlie Artful' Capstick with the task of infiltrating the underworld and gathering information about the activities of 'persistently clever and dangerous criminals'. According to Capstick:

With an outwardly battered but super-tuned family car for transport, we roamed the London jungle, making friends with the crooks, their molls, and their relatives, drinking and listening in clubs, pubs, and spielers (gambling dens), building up an army of informants which has never been equalled in the never-ending war against crime. We were not interested in the petty thieves, the small-time burglars, and the prostitutes. Our prey was the organized gangs concerned with every form of villainy from hijacking lorryloads of rationed goods to large-scale housebreaking and coupon forging.

In their first year of operation Capstick claimed they arrested 157 of the top-ranking thieves and receivers. The Ghost Squad worked from a locked office and were forbidden to talk about their work. This aroused deep suspicion among their colleagues, who suspected that the unit had been set up to examine charges of bribery and corruption

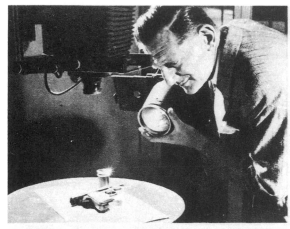

AIDS TO
DETECTION

Photography

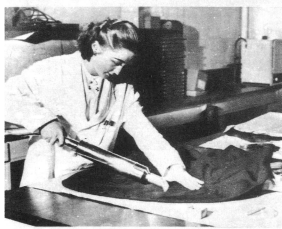

Vacuum search
for dust clues

Fingerprinting

State of the art technology.

at Scotland Yard. Ironically it was the Ghost Squad itself which became the focus for such charges. Their reliance on informers meant that they were easily tempted into acting as *agents provocateurs*. One East End trader bribed into helping was aware from his own criminal career that there were plenty of 'bad apples' in the police force. Nevertheless, he was shocked at the methods employed by this élite corps, which reported directly to the Deputy Commissioner of Scotland Yard: 'My estimation of the police fell a tremendous amount. I found they were crooked from top to bottom.' Indeed, the flurry of arrests was followed by indignant complaints about the police 'embellishing' or fabricating evidence. However, helped by such films as *The Blue Lamp* – which introduced PC George Dixon to a credulous public – and the clever self-publicization of glamorous detectives like Fabian of the Yard, the image of the police took a turn for the better. And the myth of the kindly approachable bobby on the beat and the shrewd, honest, hard-working Scotland Yard detective took a firm hold on the public imagination.

Spot Takes Over

Billy Hill, who was to develop a flair for public relations, represented the gangland feud of the late forties as a war of liberation against the race gangs who had terrorized and oppressed ordinary underworld thieves:

The generations of repression, extortion, and blackmail were remembered vividly by the sons of men who had spent years in gaol because of the race gangs. At last they saw a chance to revenge themselves for their fathers and uncles and grandfathers. I saw a chance to clean up the West End. So the Elephant mob came my way, and over the bridge from South London with them came the teams from Brixton and Camberwell and Southwark and Rotherhithe. From Shepherd's Bush and Notting Hill the burglars came, and the King's Cross gang and the Holloway team joined in. The Paddington and Kilburn lot fell in behind as well.

This gathering of the gangs owed more to the novels of Edgar Wallace than to the realities of underworld life, and it is unlikely that Hill, who had been firmly put in his place by King's Cross hit-man Eddie Raimo five years earlier, played any part in this struggle for power. It was Jack Spot, favoured by a number of wealthy bookies and backed by the ferocious gypsies of Upton Park, who represented the most powerful new force emerging in the underworld.

In a general clamp-down on illicit gambling clubs in June 1940, Spot and his cronies had been arrested and dragooned into the army. While happy enough to fight the fascists, Spot was less at home doing drill in an ill-fitting uniform at Norton Manor Barracks, Taunton. He objected to the poor pay, bad food and petty bullying inherent in army life. In the first regiment to which he was posted he got into a fight with an anti-semitic corporal, and he spent most of his service period fighting army discipline. After three years, the marine regiment he had been sent to as a last resort admitted failure and discharged him as mentally unstable.

He returned to a Blitz-devastated East End to find his parents dead and his friends and family dispersed. He involved himself in various spivish activities in the New Cross area of south-east London but remained discontented. One wet afternoon in November 1943 he was sitting in an almost deserted spieler in Paddington, mildly remonstrating with a local tough guy known as 'Edgware Road Sam' for his abuse of the Jewish barman. The argument, not unexpectedly, turned to violence and Spot, who rarely carried a weapon, smashed the gun-toting tearaway over the head with a teapot. He did rather more damage than he had meant to and was advised to make himself scarce. Sick of London anyway, he bought a platform ticket and caught a train to Leeds, the black-market capital of the north.

Leeds operated as a sort of 'open city' during the war years, a haven for deserters, a paradise for gamblers, a headquarters for racketeers. It was a world in which Spot rapidly made his mark. His fearlessness, his strength and his alcoholic abstinence gave him an advantage over the local gangsters. Before long he had reached a power-sharing arrangement with the Poles who appeared to dominate the Leeds underworld: Spot would look after the interests of bookies and club owners, while the Poles restricted their activities to taxis and petrol rationing. Spot's strong arm was welcomed by a club owner called 'Milky' (a nickname deriving from his past profession rather than the nature of his personality). As well as keeping order in his clubs, Spot accompanied the ex-milkman to the Leeds dog-racing track. Milky knew a lot about greyhounds and was a very successful bookie, but he was plagued by a former coal-

man who had adopted the name of Carl Brisson (a famous Swedish singer and film star) and wore a bowler and a pin-striped suit. His habit of placing bets but not actually putting his money in the bag was quickly terminated by Spot. Other tough guys, 'Liverpool Jack' (Jackie Bentley) and 'London Alf' (Alf Lucy), were also put in their places. Spot returned to London at the end of the war with his reputation greatly enhanced and with influential enough contacts to open a gambling club in St Botolph's Row, on the border between the City of London and the East End.

The immediate post-war period saw an unprecedented boom in gambling clubs. High wages, the profits of crime and racketeering, a live-now-pay-later attitude induced by the war, and restrictions on travel which prevented the rich spending their money in the traditional continental playgrounds, all encouraged a vigorous and varied night-life. Arthur Helliwell tantalized the readers of the *People* with a description of London's gaming clubs in 1947:

I watched gin rummy being played for £1 a point. I saw a Slippery Sam school where the kitty averaged between £200 and £250 a hand. I drank a glass of champagne with a suave, silver-haired, slickly-tailored character who takes a rake-off on a £15,000 to £20,000 turnover every time he runs a chemmy party. I visited a poker game where you couldn't see the green baize for fivers and I rounded off my tour watching a Negro dice game that shifts its rendezvous and changes its entrance pass-word every night. 'I'm driving a Ford V8' was the open sesame the night I called. There were three other white men in the dingy smoke-filled room. The rest were zoot-suited, sombrero-hatted, jazzily-necktied coloured boys. A chocolate-coloured dandy in a long black overcoat with an astrakhan collar had the dice.

Jack Spot's club was quiet and discreet, a place where serious gamblers from all walks of life, including the underworld, could meet. According to Spot:

We had a rum mixture. There were big business-men. There were bookmakers with pockets full of sucker money. There were spivs and screwsmen from the underworld getting rid of the cash they had picked up for the gear they had stolen. And of course the biggest players of all were the black-market boys.

Arthur Skurry was recruited as doorman to keep away the 'funny faces' who might cause trouble. And every Friday afternoon one of Spot's lieutenants was despatched to Water-loo station with a carrier bag full of daffodils and five-pound notes to keep a leading City of London policeman happy.

The club was owned by one of Spot's afflu-ent Jewish friends, 'a millionaire who had made his lolly in every way you can think of – and all of them bent'. But Spot was some-thing more than a front man. The club pro-vided him with a power base from which to extend his racing interests. In July 1946, with the aid of Arthur Skurry and the Upton Park gypsies, he wrested control of Ascot from Jimmy Wooder and the Islington mob. As Spot consolidated his position, he seemed to be moving towards a head-on collision with the White mob, who had dominated the English underworld since the fall of Darby Sabini.

At Yarmouth racecourse in October 1946, Spot and his men had defied White hit-man Eddie Raimo to secure a pitch for an ageing Jewish bookie, and other racecourse incidents followed. In January 1947, Spot, whose habit of drinking lemonade instead of alcohol was apt to provoke derisive comments from his enemies, followed Johnnie Warren, a cousin of the Whites, into a West End pub toilet and gave him a severe going-over. As he ex-plained to me, many years later: 'I used to knock 'em out in the lavatory, that was my surgery. I used to go into the toilet and bomp! Leave 'em in the piss.' Within minutes the Whites were on the warpath and tracked Spot down to Al Burnett's Stork Club in Sackville Street. Spot was now backed up by some of his more ferocious henchmen, and against the gentle strains of Charmian San-dler's Ladies Band, a pitched battle began. The Whites had been on top so long they had forgotten how to fight and Spot emerged the undisputed victor. He could now claim to be 'King of the Underworld', but significantly he did no such thing. After a ticking-off from the respectable businessmen and bookmakers he was associated with for disturbing the peace, he went to cool his heels in Southend – during the coldest January for over a hun-dred years.

On 13 January Arthur Helliwell reported in the *People* that in a deserted south coast seaside resort he had seen 'the notorious missing gang boss who ducked out of London a week or two ago when the heat was on'. And he warned that 'carloads of cosh- and razor-armed thugs have been searching Soho to carve him up'. But Spot was less worried about the Whites than about the police. One of the White mob, 'Big Bill' Goller, had been cut so badly that there was a danger he would die. Fortunately he pulled through and, to the disappointment of the police and the relief of the underworld, refused to name his assailants. Spot was able to return to London. It was now that the gathering of the gangs described by Hill occured, though hardly in the dramatic form he imagined. Spot was in a strong position and had every interest in keeping a low profile. Peter Beveridge, by this time a Chief Superintendent at Scotland Yard, records that the gangs

were planning to resume their fight at Harringay Arena on the night of the Baksi v. Woodcock fight [17 April 1947], so I also went along to see the leader. I had never met him before but he had a tough reputation and I expected a battle, at least of words. Instead he was very meek and mild and accepted my hint that I would view any trouble at Harringay in a very personal way. He made only one point – that I tell the other gang the same thing.

According to Spot, things were settled with the police at Savile Row police station, not at Harringay, and Inspector Bob Higgins and various other Flying Squad officers were involved, as well as Beveridge. But the important point is that, true to the British tradition of compromise, things were settled not by a bloody battle but by a quiet chat and a redrawing of boundaries – with the Whites left in control of the dog stadiums.

Alec de Antiquis dies in Charlotte Street after being shot in a bungled robbery; this picture was syndicated throughout the world.

It was just as well Spot had made his peace with the police. Less than two weeks later a motor-cyclist, Alec de Antiquis, was shot dead after a bungled robbery of a jeweller's shop in Charlotte Street. With photographs of the young man bleeding to death in the gutters of central London appearing in British and foreign newspapers, the police came under pressure to raid and harry the underworld until the killers were found. Robert Fabian and Bob Higgins, who headed the investigation, steered clear of Spot and his associates and before long discovered the culprits were a trio of small-time Bermondsey crooks, two of whom were hanged for the murder.

The 1948 airport robbery

In 1948 Heathrow airport was still in the process of construction. A huge central terminal building had been completed, but on the north side customs operations were still carried out in a collection of flimsy, temporary buildings. Sammy Josephs (known also as Sammy Ross), a well-connected Jewish thief, had discovered from a friend who worked at the airport that extremely valuable cargoes were sometimes kept there overnight.

Jack Spot's mob had worked successfully with Josephs on a series of lorry hijacks and were eager to take part in this ambitious project, though Spot himself – doing nicely from his club and the racetracks – was more circumspect. Meticulous preparations were carried out. Each of the team went on the special guided tour for visitors to the airport to familiarize themselves with the layout of the place. Bulky parcels were sent from Ireland, and Josephs and another member of the team, Franny Daniels, who were properly authorized as lorry drivers, were allowed into the inner precincts of the customs shed to collect them.

Everything was carefully planned, but the endemic danger of any such elaborate 'project crime' was that word would leak out about it. Indeed, the police had received 'certain information' that something was to happen on the night of 24 July. By 11 p.m. the roads leading to the airport were being kept under discreet observation, thirteen policemen lay in wait in the warehouse itself and ten more were hiding in a van round the back. At 11.30 things started to happen. When they heard a lorry driving up three policemen disguised as airport officials sprawled themselves out in the office, pretending they were drugged. Masked men entered, tied up the 'officials' and took their keys. One of them wasn't quite convincing enough and, although the robbers didn't yet suspect a police trap, he was coshed into genuine unconsciousness. Ten men crept stealthily towards the customs shed. Silently they followed a single torch beam towards the place where a million pounds' worth of gold ingots was supposed to be lying. They had nylon stockings over their faces and each man was armed with some sort of cosh – a lead pipe, a heavy chair leg, a car starting-crank. Suddenly all hell broke loose as what appeared to be the entire Flying Squad leapt out of the shadows towards them. A brief but bloody battle ensued before the battered robbers were dragged off into waiting Black Marias.

Jack Spot recuperating in style after the Battle of Frith Street.

The Flying Squad claimed their thwarting of the raid as a great victory, but not all the gang were captured. Teddy Machin, Spot's chiv-man, was chased by a couple of police-men and fell headlong into a deep trench. Knocked unconscious by his fall, he lay there unnoticed until the hue and cry was over and he had recovered sufficiently to stumble away to safety. Franny Daniels hid under one of the waiting Black Marias and clung to its underside by toes and fingers when it drove away, hoping to drop off at the first set of traffic lights. Unfortunately for him, with sirens blaring the police drove straight through to Harlesden police station, but some-how he hung on and managed to crawl away into the night. On the morning of 30 July 1948, the *Daily Herald* reported that:

Eight bloodstained men, alleged to have been ar-rested in a fight at a London Airport warehouse said to contain £6 million worth of diamonds and £3 million in gold, appeared in court today. The men, several of whom wore bandages and slings, were guarded by nine policemen grouped around the dock. As the men filed in, a blonde woman pushed her way into court, cried out and had to be helped out again.

Both sides knew that if the airport robbery had been successful it would have heralded a new era of large-scale 'project' crime. Thus there was not much surprise when the eight men were sentenced to a total of sixty-nine years. Sir Gerald Dodson, the Recorder of London, told them:

All of you men set your minds and hands to this enterprise. You were, of course, playing for high stakes. You made sure of your position by being ready for any situation with weapons of all kinds. This is the gravity of the offence. A raid on this scale profoundly shocks society. You went prepared for violence and you got it. You got the worst of it, and you can hardly complain.

Nothing could be proved against Jack Spot – not even that he had hidden and provided for Daniels and Machin, the two robbers who had got away. His St Botolph's Row gambling club came under such heavy police pressure it was forced to close, but Spot had a variety of other criminal interests which ensured that he remained the most powerful figure in the underworld.

9 FIFTIES CRIME

Every screwsman in history has always dreamed of the last job of all. It is the job which will be so big, so clever and so profitable that it will not be necessary ever to get his stick out again. Never again will he have to buzz a drum, screw a door, climb a ladder and blow a peter. Never again will he ever feel that awful feeling in the pit of his stomach as he stands in the dock listening to the judge doling out five of the best. This big job will solve all those problems. There will be so much ready cash in it that his friends will be looked after . . . There will be a posh drag, something like a Cadillac or a Jaguar. Suits, forty guinea suits, regular Savile Row jobs, handmade shoes and the best hotels and restaurants . . . A flat in town, plush carpets, hot and cold laid on, a manor in the country . . .

Duncan Webb, *Deadline for Crime* (1955)

Hill on the run

In his autobiography, *Boss of Britain's Underworld*, Billy Hill cheekily claims that it was he rather than Jack Spot who broke the power of the White mob. His subsequent invisibility is explained by the fact that 'even before the tumult had died down and the big hush had set in, Nemesis greeted me with a hollow laugh, and I was nicked again'. Nemesis was no stranger to the Hill household, but this was a 'you'll do' case of Hill being in the wrong place at the wrong time, and he resented going back inside for a crime he didn't commit. After being granted bail, he went on the run. Having talked things over with his wife, Aggie, he considered leaving Britain for ever.

It would mean turning my back on London for good and all. It would mean goodbye to the Big Smoke, farewell to Odd Legs, Tosh, Franny, Horrible Harry, Taters Mutton and all the boys. I wondered if I could stand the severance of not being with Strong Arms again, or Wide Gaiters Alf, or Long Stan or Big Jock.

But the spectre of Dartmoor was enough to banish Hill's sentimental scruples and he decided he might enjoy life outside England.

He and 'John the Tilter' (John Tilly, a West London garage owner later suspected of grassing on the airport robbers) pretended they were detectives and relieved a couple of crooks of their haul of stolen parachutes. With the £9,225 they gained for their endeavour, Hill took off for South Africa. In Johannesburg he teamed up with British boxer and villain Bobby Ramsay and opened a gambling club. But this brought him into conflict with the South African 'Guv'nor of Guv'nors', Arnold Neville, a seventeen stone all-in wrestler. Hill believed that 'in the underworld if you take a step backwards, that step invariably becomes a bit of a push until you're going backwards all the time', and when Neville and his men arrived to smash up the club they got more than they bargained for. The *Rand Daily Mail* reported the following day that the former wrestler had needed nearly a hundred stitches after being attacked outside a city night-club.

His assailants slashed his head and buttocks with razors and his condition is serious. It is alleged that shots were fired during the attack. At about 1.30 a.m. Neville and two friends were standing outside the night-club when there was an argument. Blows were struck. Two men drew razors and one a revolver. Neville's friends retreated. When Neville attempted to break away, he was knocked to the ground and slashed.

Hill was arrested in a hideout in Durban and brought back to Johannesburg for trial. His respectable demeanour – horn-rimmed spectacles and a dark suit – impressed the judge and he was granted bail. Gangland quarrels were lightly regarded by the South African courts and Hill would probably have had to serve only a few months in prison. But he knew that such a sentence would inevitably be followed by extradition to England and arrest on the charge over which he had jumped bail. Once again he went on the run and decided to make his own way back to England.

Discreetly avoiding his usual haunts, Hill holed up in East Ham, part of the territory controlled by the Upton Park mob. In September

1947 he carried out a robbery in Manchester with two of Jack Spot's associates, Sammy Josephs and Teddy Machin, carrying off a bookmaker's safe containing £9,000. The English underworld was too small, though, for a well-known villain to remain incognito for long and, rather than wait for the inevitable, he gave himself up and was sentenced to three years in Wandsworth.

The Spot–Hill alliance

It was late in 1949 that Hill, after gaining full remission on his sentence, emerged from the prison gates to be met by Jack Spot. He was middle-aged, penniless and 'as thin as a pickled herring', according to Spot, but he was known and trusted by several of the airport robbers, and Spot recruited him as a lieutenant to replace those he had lost. Spot was the most powerful British gangster since Darby Sabini, and whereas Sabini's influence was confined to London and the racecourses of southern England, Spot's wartime sojourn in Leeds had made him a power to be reckoned with in the north too.

Hill was, undeniably, a useful ally. He was reliable and steadfast and respected as being a successful crook, despite his seventeen years in jail. The 1948 Criminal Justice Act, though ostensibly a reforming measure, had brought in new provisions to make more widespread use of preventive detention. If Hill was caught again, as a habitual criminal, he could expect an extra ten years PD to be added to his sentence. Thus he determined to find less risky ways of making a living. Spot offered him the chance of looking after spielers.

Spielers, semi-legal gambling clubs, had been around before the war but then they had been small-scale and predominantly ethnic. The illicit profits of the black market caused a boom for the clubs during the war which continued into the fifties. According to Sammy Samuels, who ran small Soho clubs from the thirties to the sixties:

The gaming clubs and the drinking clubs in and around Soho are meeting places for the fly-boys, the screwsmen and the tea-leafs, the hustlers and the sharpers, and while on the one hand the club guv'nor can do without their custom he cannot keep them out of the club. They are part of the set-up. That they may bring trouble with them is one of those things a gaming club guv' has to face.

This was one of the reasons why partnership with a powerful underworld figure was not just a matter of parasitism. A character like Spot or Hill was able to ensure that order would be kept, and that large amounts of money could change hands without the winner fearing for his safety. Spielers served as social clubs for the underworld. As Hill explained:

They do not have names and committees and all that stuff. They just start, usually in a cellar or any suitable premises that can be found, and the word gets round that there's a game on. Then the customers come in. They range from regular villains and tearaways to every kind of person from titled aristocrats down to cab-drivers and waiters. We never did allow any steamers in. Our game was not to trim mugs who wanted to play for some sort of thrill. There was no need for that.

Poker, faro, chemin-de-fer and various forms of rummy were played for high stakes. It was part of the underworld ethos to spend freely and most crooks went through their ill-gotten gains rapidly and conspicuously rather than investing them for future respectability. There are stories – possibly apocryphal – of gambling-mad burglars like 'Taters' Chatham absenting themselves from a game for a couple of hours and returning with replenished funds after a profitable venture into Mayfair – and then losing everything in the course of the night.

Fights were not frequent but when they did occur they tended to be ferocious. Jackie Reynolds, one of the Upton Park gypsies, ran a very successful club in Southend. But business was disrupted when his croupier, a retired Portuguese Jewish boxer ('built like a tank') called Arraller aroused the distrust of Benny Swann, the leader of the gypsies who worked the Kursaal fairground. Memories of their fight had hardly died down when Reynolds himself was involved in a bloody battle with the sallow, lugubrious chiv-man Teddy Machin. An observer commented that they were 'like two mad fucking dogs fighting each other. You couldn't part them.' A feared and respected 'guv'nor' tended to deter such disturbances.

Cold, hard and unchatty, with totally expressionless eyes ('it was like looking into black glass'), Hill was hardly a convivial host. But he had followed Spot's example in not drinking alcohol and he was adept at keeping order with a minimum of fuss. Also, he was a good gambler, with a sixth sense about the draw and fall of a card. Sammy Samuels

A model young mother: Rita Comer with her two daughters.

claims that Hill 'set a tone of play and conduct which has not been equalled', that he dominated a table 'through sheer gambling ability' and that as long as the game was fast and fair he never made a fuss about losing. 'Where another man would turn nasty over a losing run, Bill simply shrugged.'

Spot had spent most of the nights of his youth hanging around late-night drinking and gambling clubs. But by the early fifties he too was ready for a change of lifestyle. In June 1951, at Haydock Park races, he met Rita, a young Irish girl who was to become his wife. She later told a newspaper that, having won £50 in a competition, she gave half to her mother and on the other half came to Liverpool to have some fun.

I looked around for the nicest-looking bookmaker. Someone I could trust. Then I saw him. Broad-shouldered, expensively dressed – master of all around him. I went across. I looked appealingly into his eyes. He met my gaze. 'Could I have ten shillings each way?' I asked him. I had FALLEN IN LOVE WITH JACK SPOT.

He wooed her assiduously, showering her with gifts and following her back to Dublin. As Rita recalled: 'He was good to Mum so I married him.'

Hill and Spot acted together with speed and efficiency when curbing unrest. Their old enemy, Harry White, after being squeezed out from the racecourses, attempted to take over the protection rackets at London's grey-hound stadiums, but he came into conflict with 'Ginger' Rumble and his Shepherd's Bush Boys. Hill and Spot all but kidnapped the two men and forced them to agree on a truce and an equitable division of the spoils. Looking back, Spot thought he had been too soft. 'I made a mistake. I let the fucking King's Cross mob come back. I should have wiped them out.' But the King's Cross–Islington–Clerkenwell nexus was impossible to eradicate from the London underworld.

Hill prospered, but his propensity for vio-lence caused his partner considerable embar-rassment. He had formed an attachment to Gypsy Riley, a tempestuous good-time girl, and Gypsy's hot temper and foul mouth led Hill into actions which he later regretted. 'Belgian Johnny', a Belgian Jewish refugee who had turned to pimping as a means of making a living in England had had dealings with Gypsy in the past. Indignantly, the woman who now liked to regard herself as 'Queen of the Underworld' complained to Hill that Johnny wanted to put her back on the game. Hill remedied this affront to her dignity by marching into the West End restaurant where the Belgian refugees congregated and slashing Johnny about the face and neck. The first Spot knew about the incident was when he picked up the phone to hear a worried Hill imploring him to go to the Char-ing Cross hospital and see if the badly injured Belgian could be straightened. Spot obliged. Johnny had learnt the rules of the English underworld sufficiently to forgive and forget – for a price – but he was being put in a difficult position. The police were threatening that unless he named his assailant he would be deported. Spot apologized, upped the stakes a bit and advised him not to name Hill. Belgian Johnny went back to Belgium.

Apart from incidents like this, the under-world was running smoothly and Spot de-cided it might calm Gypsy and Hill down if they went on holiday. So, accompanied by his young Irish wife, he took them off to the south of France. To Hill, who had never been further than the Isle of Wight, the good life on the Riviera was a revelation and he deter-mined to make up for all those lost years in cold, damp cells. As he wrote later:

The sun was soothing now. Its warmth was caress-ing my limbs and back, ironing out the sores which had always been there from those baskets full of stone. Then it was beating down on my face, softening the chiv scars and penetrating my mind and easing the bitterness of porridge and cocoa, of the stench of Wandsworth, the mildew of the Moor, the odour of grey, dark prisons which destroy men and devour their humanity. There was a warmth and softness in my life. Not again, for it had never been there before. It was new to me, this comfort and solace, this easing of the burden which had rounded the shoulders of my mind through the years.

When they returned, Spot made ready for his retirement. On 13 October 1951 Arthur Helliwell announced in the *People* that he had had a visit from 'Britain's Al Capone, the self-confessed Czar of Gangland'.

After nearly twenty-five years as a mobster, he has finally reached the conclusion that crime doesn't pay! He walked into my office with two bodyguards and announced his intention of quitting the shady side of the street and going into what he calls 'legit business'. No one knows who the next Big Shot will be – but I don't need a crystal ball to predict that in the months following his retirement the streets of Soho, the racetracks and gambling dens will be decidedly unhealthy spots.

Helliwell was obviously unaware that Billy Hill was waiting in the wings, and had Spot carried through his intention the events of the mid-fifties might have been less dramatic. Instead, a power-sharing arrangement was worked out. Spot would maintain his presence on the racetracks while Hill concentrated on the spielers.

Both areas were to be squeezed as calls came to close down disreputable gambling dens and clean up the racecourses in the lead-up to the Betting and Gaming Act of 1960. But Soho's spielers presented a much less public face than the goings-on at racetracks. The Jockey Club and the big credit bookmakers like William Hill (no relation) and Ladbrokes made a powerful lobby with a vested interest in showing how betting on horses was a respectable activity which would be well served by legitimate off-course betting shops.

Ironically Spot himself played a useful role in keeping order on the racecourses, negotiating between Jockey Club stewards like Lord Rosebery and the Duke of Norfolk and the slightly dubious bookmakers who set up their pitches on the free side of courses such as Epsom and Ascot. However, the racecourse authorities were themselves taking an increasingly active role in regulating and licensing bookmakers, and by the mid-fifties Spot and his fellow racing gangsters were only able to command a rake-off from bookmakers working at the small, amateur, point-to-point meetings, where crowds – and the proceeds from betting – were much smaller. Thus Spot found himself a boss of the underworld with a steadily diminishing power base and a wily and unscrupulous partner who was more open than he was to new opportunities.

As a keen gambler whose marriage had finally died during his last spell inside, Hill took to the spielers like a duck to water. He was reticent and reserved but he enjoyed being surrounded by people and was always willing to listen to them, carefully storing the information for future use. It was in these underworld spielers that alliances were made, jobs discussed, gossip exchanged and plots hatched. Hill soon found opportunities for putting such information to good use.

A Soho street in the fifties.

Vice in London

One area neither Spot nor Hill was anxious to move into was vice. Since the murder of the mysterious Latvian Emil Allard in 1936, the vice scene had been dominated by five brothers of mixed Egyptian, Sicilian and Maltese descent – Attilio, Carmelo, Alfredo, Eugenio and Salvatore Messina. The number of prostitutes in London tripled during the war, and the Messinas took full advantage of the increase in demand. As the French prostitute Marthe Watts explained: 'London became filled with British and Allied troops and with war workers away from home. Time was short, money was loose, morals were out.' The Messinas made their women work strictly regulated hours, starting at four o'clock in the afternoon and working through until six the following morning, and spending a maximum of ten minutes with a customer, which frequently left them unsatisfied and quarrelsome. Watts reckoned that she earned £150,000 for 'Gino' Messina between 1940 and 1955. She was exceptionally industrious, managing to get through forty-nine men on VE Day, but the profits to be made from prostitution were making it an increasingly important source of underworld income.

Before the war many prostitutes solicited around Marble Arch and the Bayswater Road and used Hyde Park for their liaisons – thus sparing themselves the expense of West End accommodation. In the blackout the whole of London served as Hyde Park, with couples copulating undisturbed in the darkness. When the lights came on again there was pressure to clean up this very public display of sex. The number of prostitutes diminished as husbands returned from overseas service and good-time girls became respectable housewives. But the broadening of sexual experience which occurred during the war and the increased level of prosperity led to a permanent increase in the demands for illicit sex. Paradoxically, though, there was a strong emphasis on respectability and conformity in the fifties, as people tried to settle down and forget the trauma of war, and a public and open market for sex seemed to cause much more offence than it had done in the pre-war period. The Conservative MP for Southend, Sir Beverley Baxter, complained of the 'guard of dishonour' which occupied the pavements from Park Lane to Marble Arch, and newspapers attacked 'the ghastly army of prostitutes who infest our streets'. The campaign was led not by the right-wing press but by the *Daily Mirror* and the *People*, which combined a robust populism with a puritanical contempt for decadence and corruption. Thus it was not altogether surprising that, with Hill and Spot wary of interfering and the police bought off, the dissolution of the Messina ring should have been left to an eccentric young reporter.

Duncan Webb

Thomas Duncan Webb began his career in journalism as a cub reporter on the *South London Press* in the thirties and showed an aptitude for crime stories. When war broke out he joined up and served in West Africa before being invalided out in 1944. He worked on the *Daily Express* under Arthur

Christiansen, and then moved on to the *Evening Standard*, where his obsession with crime reporting made him an uncomfortable colleague. After a row with his editor he left.

One of the reasons I left . . . was that my superiors claimed it was not the business of a newspaper to go prying into the affairs of corpses with no arms. Lady So-and-So, the wife of the proprietor, would not like it, I was told. They pooh-poohed the idea. 'We are a respectable newspaper,' they said. 'After all, murders are so vulgar.'

Fortunately Webb found a less squeamish editor in Sam Campbell, who was then attempting to revive the fortunes of the *People* with daring, controversial journalism. Even on crime stories Webb had not officially covered, such as the sex murders carried out by Neville George Heath in June 1946 and the Antiquis affair of May 1947, he had compiled dossiers and offered (unwanted) advice to the police. In 1949 there were two sensational murder cases which allowed Webb full scope for his talents.

Webb remembered John George Haigh's name from his (unproved) association with the corpse with no arms to which the *Evening Standard* had been so indifferent. He was now accused of murdering a series of well-off middle-aged ladies whom he had befriended. Since Haigh had already obliged the police with a detailed confession of how he drank a pint of blood from his victims' bodies before dissolving them in a vat of sulphuric acid, there was little doubt about his guilt. But Webb dredged up some fascinating background detail. He found that Haigh frequented many of the pubs which Webb him-

self – and another murderer, Neville Heath – used: the Goat in Kensington, the Trevor Arms and the Nag's Head in Knightsbridge. He became friendly with Haigh's young fiancée and was told about the considerate, gentle side of the murderer's nature. He discovered that Haigh had a wife who was living in happy bigamy in Cornwall and persuaded her to legitimize her union by remarrying immediately after her husband's execution. The following Sunday photographs of the wedding – with Webb as best man – appeared in the *People*.

On 22 October, shortly after Mrs Haigh's wedding, another limbless torso made an appearance. Essex wildfowler Sidney Tiffin discovered the body of Stanley Setty, a Warren Street car dealer, washed up on the Tillingham marshes. He had been missing since 4 October and his brother-in-law had offered a £1,000 reward. Thirteen stone 'Honest Stan', who was involved in currency and coupon frauds and gun-running to Palestine as well as dubious dealings with cars, had many enemies. It was thought at first that a Jewish terrorist group had decided to pay him back for short-changing them. But the man who was arrested was a small-time spiv called Donald Hume, who had procured stolen cars and disposed of forged petrol coupons for Setty. Webb knew Hume vaguely as a denizen of the murky clubs and flashy pubs patronized by the underworld and the glitterati. But it was only after the trial, when he became Mrs Hume's lover, that he was convinced of his guilt. By that time Hume had been acquitted of murder but sentenced to twelve years' imprisonment as an acces-

An unlikely alliance: night-club hostess and murderer's wife, Cynthia Hume, and crusading reporter, Thomas Duncan Webb.

sory after the fact. Mrs Hume obtained a divorce and continued her liaison with Webb.

While he was courting Cynthia Hume, Webb was given a new assignment by his editor: to discover exactly what the Messina brothers were up to and to expose it to the light of day. 'Smash this gang of ponces,' he was told. 'So I smashed it. And I drove the fragments whence they came; back to the brothels and gutters of the back streets of Europe.' But the Messinas proved to be a formidable enemy.

Smashing the ponces

For three weeks Webb scoured the underworld, trying to piece together a picture of the Messinas and their operation. He discovered that in 1934 Eugenio, the brightest of Mrs and Mrs Giuseppe Messina's five sons, had come to England. His family had run brothels in Sicily, Malta, Egypt, Morocco and Spain, so it was hardly surprising that Eugenio should put his wife on the streets of London. He found he could make a good living, and before long brought over his brothers to help build a vice empire. According to Webb:

By bribery and corruption they organized marriages of convenience both in Britain and abroad to enable their harlots to assume British nationality. They ruled their women by persuasion, threat, or blackmail and the use of the knife and the razor. They ruled the streets of the West End by similar methods. Indeed, so terror-stricken did the underworld become at the mention of the word 'Messina' that in the end they found little difficulty in building up their vast empire of vice.

The average crook was reluctant to say anything very specific about the Messinas and Webb needed more than vague insinuations. He decided to try a more direct approach. Posing as a punter looking for a good time, he allowed himself to be picked up by prostitutes. He told English women who seemed to have no links with the Messinas he was a journalist and tried – without much success – to enlist their help. He had to be more circumspect with the foreign prostitutes he suspected of working for the Messinas, concealing his identity while trying to learn as much as possible before making an excuse and leaving.

He was frequently unable to extract himself without embarrassment. A French prostitute called Violet merely told him to 'Get out!' when he offered her a fiver to let him stay all night. But then he was approached by another Frenchwoman in Shepherd's Market: 'She was tall, and extremely fat. Over her shoulder fox furs were draped. Her jet-black hair, parted in the centre, was swept back. Her lips were thick. She took me into a flat at 49a Hertford Street.' When Webb gave one of his weaker excuses he got more than he bargained for: 'When I offered this woman ten shillings, she literally roared. She spat at me through clenched teeth. Even on the lower deck in the Navy I had never heard such a torrent of obscene blasphemy.'

Webb made a rapid exit, with the Frenchwoman bellowing obscenities after him. He thought it would be a good idea to keep away from Shepherd's Market for a while and turned his attention to Bond Street. But once again his charm proved unequal to the occasion. When taken to a room in Stafford Street by a tall, fair-haired Swiss woman called Jean, he told her he had changed his mind. 'She spat at me, aimed several blows at me, and pushed me towards the door. As I was about to descend the stairs, she gave me a violent kick in the back . . .' Webb persisted, however, and over a period of a fortnight reckoned he was picked up by almost a hundred women. As yet there was nothing to connect them with the Messinas, but, posing as a property developer, he discovered who owned or leased the houses to which he had been taken by the prostitutes. Five names – Marshall, Maitland, Evans, Maynard and Martin – cropped up repeatedly and Webb's first real break-through was the discovery that these were aliases for Eugenio, Carmelo, Salvatore, Attilio and Alfredo Messina.

He was able to convince Campbell that he had the essence of a really big story – the biggest crime story since William Stead exposed the child prostitution racket in the columns of the *Pall Mall Gazette* in the 1880s – and he was given several helpers. Apart from learning how to make an excuse and leave when confronted with an irate prostitute, they were given the task of following each of the Messina brothers and establishing their links with the girls on the streets.

By this time the Messinas were aware that something was afoot. Eugenio had served a three-year sentence in 1947 for stabbing a rival Maltese ponce in the stomach, and the

Webb's exposé: headlines from the *People*, 3 September 1950.

brothers were determined not to involve themselves personally in physical violence again. But their women felt no such scruples and, armed with the spiked umbrellas which were their trademark, they could be dangerous. Webb was repeatedly attacked by Marthe Watts, who had 'Gino le Maltaise, homme de ma vie' tattooed on her left breast to betoken her loyalty to her protector. At one point he was besieged in a pub by Watts and two other Messina women, Blanche Costarki and Marie Sanderson. After waiting an hour and a half, he ordered a taxi and decided to run for it: 'The distance from the door of the bar to the taxi was probably two and a half yards. Yet as I leaped over that distance, dozens of blows rained upon my head, neck, and shoulders. My spectacles were knocked off, and Watts tried to tear the lapel of my jacket.'

Taking photographs aroused particular hostility. Webb's usual photographer, a small but far from timid man called Bill Breeze, survived being knocked down in the street by Marthe Watts and Blanche Costarki, but after being chased by Violet Carter, Jeanne Connolly and a crowd of bloodthirsty onlookers, he decided he'd had enough. He was replaced by Stan Jaanus, a tough Bermondsey lad who had learnt his craft photographing drunks in the pubs of south London and was afraid of no one.

Webb's flat in Brunswick Square was now being kept under constant observation, though he rarely slept there. Going back one Friday night to change his clothes he was nearly caught by Messina heavies and only

Alfredo (left) and Attilio Messina.

escaped because he had taken the precaution of asking his taxi-driver to wait and keep his engine running. Driven at great speed to Euston, Webb jumped on to a train pulling out of the station and spent the early hours of the morning wandering around Luton. Nevertheless, despite intimidation, police corruption and treachery among jealous colleagues, he completed his research and on 3 September 1950 the *People* appeared with a banner headline demanding: ARREST THESE FOUR MEN. Webb had not yet unmasked Alfredo, but there were pictures of Eugenio, Carmelo, Attilio and Salvatore, captioned: 'They are the Emperors of a vice Empire in the heart of London.' It was the first in a series of sensational exposés of the vice scene.

Webb's success depended on his ingenuity and dogged persistence, but he was also fortunate in attracting the support of Billy Hill, who, like many 'old school' criminals, didn't like ponces and didn't like foreigners. He was happy to see Webb break the power of the Messinas and he was able to call on the support of a considerable army of heavies. On the morning that the first article appeared, the five angry brothers stormed into the Brunswick Arms, Webb's local, to find him chatting casually at the bar with Billy Hill. An assortment of rough-looking men, distinctly out of place in this middle-class Bloomsbury pub, turned to greet them with hostile stares as they entered. Henceforth Webb had the freedom of the underworld and he and Hill struck up a deep, and mutually useful, friendship. Without Hill's support Webb would never have been able to break down the protection the Messinas enjoyed

and bring them to court. Without Webb, who wrote about him frequently and sympathetically and ghosted his autobiography, *Boss of Britain's Underworld*, Hill would have remained as shadowy a figure as the gang bosses of the twenties and thirties.

Webb's reports on the activities of the Messina brothers provoked considerable interest. Marthe Watts reported: 'People came from here, there and everywhere to watch us and look at the houses, as if it were a pilgrimage ... On Saturday and Sunday men, women and the children as well gathered to admire us and watch our movements.' Questions were asked in the House of Commons and the Messinas appeared to have recruited an unlikely ally in the Home Secretary, Mr Chuter Ede. Nevertheless, a police investigation was launched under Superintendent Guy Mahon which eventually led to the arrest, trial and conviction of Alfredo and Attilio Messina. The other brothers – Eugenio, Carmelo and Salvatore – fled to Europe, with Webb in pursuit. After tracking them through Paris, Marseilles, Milan, Pau, Cannes, Nice, San Remo, Turin and Genoa (where he had his hotel room rifled and his money and passport stolen) he arrived at Milan again to find 'Eugenio and Carmelo Messina strolling out of the Hotel Grand Duomo, impeccably dressed, each wearing solitaire diamond rings. They were known there as "very good respectable English *gentlemans*".' Fortunately for his health, he did not confront them. But he was able to establish that they were recruiting new girls, and that they still controlled vice operations in London through loyal female lieutenants like Marthe Watts. Back at home, Webb continued to ferret out the Messinas' agents and successors – Tony Micallef, Joseph Grech, Mark Langtry, Paul Cambridge Grubb, Maurey Conley and Antonio ('Hyena of Soho') Rossi.

Webb's attitude to law and order and the underworld was profoundly ambivalent. His cynicism about the integrity of the police didn't preclude friendship with Superintendent Herbert Sparks, who was head of the CID at West End Central between 1954 and 1958. And his hostility towards the vice racketeers has to be balanced against his respect for that semi-mythical élite of the underworld, the 'Heavy Mob'. According to Webb:

Rarely will they take money or goods from those who cannot afford it. Frequently they act the Robin Hood by giving freely to the poor and less fortunate. They have their own rules, a very strict code of honour, much ability, and a suspicion of anyone who is not as they are.

The epitome of these underworld virtues for Webb was Billy Hill: 'a crook, a villain, a thief, a thug', who he also saw as 'a genius and a kind and tolerant man'.

The 1952 mailbag robbery

With Jack Spot's help, Hill had got off the treadmill of having to 'graft' continually to keep himself and his hangers-on in funds. The 1948 Criminal Justice Act had a profound effect on underworld attitudes. The sort of two- to five-year sentences men like Hill had received in the thirties and forties for their criminal endeavours were regarded as an occupational hazard. Now, as continual reoffenders, they could expect to have another eight to ten years' preventive detention added to their sentence. This naturally made them more cautious and prompted a change towards bigger, more carefully planned robberies which offered greater rewards and which took longer to plan. In between times it was very useful to be employed in some sort of capacity – croupier, doorman, barman, driver, bodyguard – in the night-clubs and spielers.

There was a change from 'buyer'-backed crime, with its emphasis on jewellery and furs (for which the buyer would pay only a small percentage of its value) to 'project' crimes, financed by the men who carried them out and generally directed at easily disposed-of money or bullion. Criminologist Steve Chibnall, discussing the changing nature of crime in the fifties, argues that the characteristic unit of organization changed from the 'craft team' of pickpockets, burglars and small-scale robbers to the 'mob' of friends and associates involved in protection rackets, gambling, prostitution and fraud. He asserts that 'the mobs formed the recruiting ground for "project thefts" – lorry hijacking, pay-roll snatches, bank robberies etc. – which became an increasingly important part of the crime scene in the fifties'. There is a degree of simplification here, but Chibnall grasps the essential point that old barriers between different sections of the underworld were breaking down. Thieves remained thieves and protection racketeers continued to rely on extortion. But the new sort of 'mobster', like Hill, recruited men with all sorts of underworld talents.

Duncan Webb and Billy Hill.

Hill wanted to use the expertise he had picked up over the past twenty years to make a couple of good killings before he retired. The mailbag robbery carried out in Eastcastle Street early on the morning of 21 May 1952 netted £287,000 in used bank-notes, which in 1952 was an awful lot of money, and it is generally assumed that Hill was responsible for it. He writes:

Walk through Old Compton Street, or down Wardour Street, or over the heath at Newmarket on any racing day, or along the promenade at Brighton any week, and ask anyone who thinks they know. Ask them who planned the Big Mailbag Job. The one when £287,000 in freely negotiable currency notes, in hard cash, was nicked, in May 1952, and they'll all tell you, 'We don't know who did it but we've got a good idea. In any case, we do know that Billy Hill planned it. Only he could have done that.'

After seventeen years inside, Hill had learnt the necessity of patience. It took him over a year to establish a network of contacts in the post office who could provide him with the right sort of information without themselves knowing what it would be used for. He discovered that large amounts of money were collected from west country banks, carried by train to Paddington Station and driven from there to the sorting office at St Martin-le-Grand, near the Old Bailey. Some of the notes were sent to the Bank of England for pulping, others were transferred to banks in the City. Although the run from Paddington was in the early hours of the morning, most of it was along broad, well-lit streets where an ambush would be difficult to arrange. The best place Hill could think of was the tail-end of New Oxford Street, where the van left the the mainstream of traffic going down Bloomsbury Way (impossible now as the one-way flow is in the opposite direction). Then the robbers had a stroke of luck. For a short while in May 1952, roadworks closed part of Oxford Street and traffic was diverted along Eastcastle Street, a narrow back street with conveniently located mews in which block and getaway cars could be hidden. The other problem that had vexed Hill – how to silence the alarm – was dealt with by arranging for the wires to be cut before the van began its run. As this was the only way of stopping the alarm, there was no procedure for testing it.

According to Webb, the raid took place at seventeen minutes past four on the morning of 21 May and took seven minutes – an agonizingly long time for such a hijack. (When Webb came to ghost *Boss of Britain's Underworld* it had been reduced to twenty seconds.) The mail van was driven to Augustus Street, behind Mornington Crescent, a stone's throw from Netley Street, where Hill was born, and hidden in an enclosed yard. A lorry loaded with empty apple crates was concealed there and the contents of eighteen of the mailbags were transferred to a space that had been left in the middle of them. The robbers had been expecting to steal around £40,000–50,000 and they had not left enough room for such a huge haul. Hill curtly ordered that thirteen of the mailbags be left in the post office van. Rather than run the risk of passing through a police cordon, the fruit lorry was driven to Spitalfields fruit market where (usually contradictory sources Duncan Webb and Jack Spot both insist) it was left under careful observation for twenty-four hours before being driven out to Dagenham marshes for the slaughter.

The careful planning of the raid convinced some newspaper reporters that it was planned by an ex-commando officer. Webb maintained a discreet silence and an internal memo reveals that the *Daily Mirror* suspected 'Jack Sprott', as they mistakenly called him, though these suspicions were never actually published. Questions were asked in the House of Commons and Sir Winston Churchill himself stressed the importance of urgent action to catch the culprits. When Chief Superintendent Tom Barratt failed to get results he was superseded by Chief Superintendent Bob Lee, who had not only led the ambush of the

The mail van hijacked in Eastcastle Street was discovered in a yard in
Augustus Street, Mornington Crescent.

1948 airport robbers but warned Hill off from attempting a £7 million postage stamp heist during the war.

The underworld in the fifties was small and close-knit. Everyone knew everyone else and when a big job was pulled off it was almost impossible to keep secret who was involved. A policeman with good informers could learn a lot. But, as Duncan Webb comments: 'Chief Superintendent Lee learnt the names of the men who actually did the robbery. He learnt who had organized it, how it was done; but, he could not prove that even one of the men was there.' Rumours of police collusion persisted – in the underworld at least – and the robbers insisted that they left one more bag in the mail van than the police said they found. But such claims are impossible to substantiate.

After the 1952 mailbag robbery Hill never had to worry about money again. He did pull off other robberies but he meticulously covered his tracks and never went to prison again. However, the mailbag robbery strained relations with the police and Spot and Hill found their activities subjected to uncomfortably close scrutiny. For a time they ran a lavish West End club in Ham Yard (opposite the Windmill), but the police were not prepared to permit such high-profile activities. And the once-still waters of the fifties underworld were further disturbed when Gypsy Riley provoked a gangland fight which very nearly ended in murder.

Gypsy's early history is shrouded in mystery but reliable sources linked her with an ageing Maltese pimp known as Tulip. It was an association she was keen to repudiate, and when her one-time protector approached her in a night-club she encouraged Slip Sullivan, who worked for Hill as a croupier, to throw him down the stairs. Unfortunately for Sullivan, the old man, aware that he could no longer stand up for himself, employed a ferocious Hackney tearaway, Tommy Smithson, to defend him. Sullivan got rather more than he bargained for and the furious Gypsy demanded that Hill avenge the liberty taken on 'poor Slip'. Again Spot was called in and he contacted Smithson. At Hill's request, they

Tommy Smithson: 'He was as harmless as a day-old chick' (Sammy Samuels).

met round the back of the Black Cat Cigarette factory at Mornington Crescent. Smithson arrived, accompanied by his Luger and club-owner Dave Barry. Spot and his lieutenant Moisha Blueball (Morris Goldstein) came with Hill. Spot explained to Smithson that they were there to talk and persuaded him to hand over his gun (which would have been of little use as he had forgotten to buy bullets for it) and, just as he was putting it in his pocket, Hill viciously chivved the unguarded Smithson. Everyone was shocked, even Hill, who turned as white as a sheet as he realized he might have killed his victim. Barry ran away, Spot attempted to stem the bleeding and sent Moisha Blueball for an ambulance before driving Hill to his flat. Fortunately Smithson didn't die and he was not interested in co-operating with the police. Spot gave him £1,000 and promised to open a night-club for him. Smithson accepted but warned him – as Belgian Johnny had done earlier – not to trust 'that rat Billy Hill'. Within six months, however, Hill had become powerful enough to manage without Spot.

That summer, 1953, Smithson had befriended two young men who had walked out on their National Service and were trying to steer clear of the East End haunts where they would be instantly recognized. They were twins, Ronnie and Reggie Kray. Smithson found them useful to have around the billiard hall he had opened in Archer Street and allowed them to sleep on the tables when everyone had gone home. Their polite deferential manner and their utter fearlessness marked them out from other young tearaways. Spot and Hill were favourably impressed, but saw no immediate use for them. Soon they had disappeared from the scene again, serving out the remainder of their National Service in army prisons.

The Flamingo affair

Just before Christmas 1953 Hill had slashed the face of another Camden Town gangster, Freddy Andrews. At first it seemed that Andrews would break the underworld code and collaborate with the police, so, fearing a sentence of preventive detention, Hill made plans to leave England. He had begun frequenting a pub called the Star in Belgrave Square, where the landlord, Paddy Kennedy, played host to aberrant playboys, keen newspapermen, adventurous Hooray Henries and the sleeker varieties of criminal. There he teamed up with Eddie Chapman, who had moved on from safe-breaking to clever, and only marginally criminal, business deals. Hill and Chapman bought an ex-naval cruiser, renamed it *The Flamingo* and prepared to leave for Tangier. By February, when the case came to trial, Hill had sorted out his differences with Andrews, who refused to confirm that Hill was his attacker. The Recorder, Sir Gerald Dodson, told the jury that they might think that Andrews 'is either scared out of his life or is wilfully concealing the truth', but they had no choice but to find Hill not guilty.

Hill and Chapman proceeded with their plans to base themselves in Tangier and participate in the lucrative smuggling rackets carried out from the port – and they took Andrews along as a member of the crew. In the early fifties Tangier was still a free city, governed by an intenational commission with representatives from France, Spain, Portugal, Italy, Belgium and Britain. Little attempt was made to stamp out smuggling.

According to crime reporter Laurence Wilkinson:

The export of cigarettes from Tangier is perfectly legal, and the traffic is one on which the local administration relies for revenue. The transfer of these cigerettes at sea to another vessel is, likewise, legal, provided that the transfer occurs outside of territorial limits. The fact that the second vessel then runs the gauntlet of Customs patrols to land its cargo without payment of duty is considered a matter of interest only to the last two parties concerned.

On board *The Flamingo*: Billy Hill (in dark blazer) and Eddie Chapman (with white shirt and tie).

There was vicious rivalry among the smuggling gangs, however, and shortly before Hill and Chapman arrived, the activities of 'Nylon Sid' Paley and Elliott Forrest had resulted in gang warfare which had led to at least ten murders. The voyage of *The Flamingo* attracted a considerable amount of press attention and brought unwelcome publicity to the dubious activities emanating from Tangier. Duncan Webb in the *People* and Ken Smith in the *Sunday Chronicle* represented Hill, Chapman and their crew – which included Franny Daniels, Patsy 'Golden Hands' Murphy and the boxer Georgie Walker – as modern buccaneers. Much was made of an ambitious plot involving Hill kidnapping the Sultan of Morocco, who had been imprisoned by the French in Madagascar, and putting him back on his throne. But the plot never came near to being realized and the impression that comes across from the accounts written by Hill and Chapman is of a bunch of bigoted Englishmen coping badly with the problems of being abroad and the perils of the sea.

Spot and Hill fall out

Hill was much happier pulling off another big robbery on 21 September 1954. A lorry belonging to KLM, the Dutch airlines, was hijacked during rush hour outside their offices in Jockey's Fields, a narrow street off Theobalds Road, Holborn. The robbers got away with two boxes containing £45,500 in gold bullion. The getaway van was discovered in nearby Queen Square, but finding the perpetrators of the robbery was another matter. Hill was inevitably the prime suspect and an East End warehouse he owned as a venture into straight business was raided and searched systematically. It contained 20,000 toys, all in separate cardboard boxes. Hill witnessed the scene:

They were swarming in dozens in the warehouse, opening every box and closely examining every talking doll and teddy bear. As they held up the dolls to look at them they murmured 'Aah' and as they turned over the teddy bears they grunted 'Ooh'. In the end the place sounded like a blinking zoo with all the 'oohs' and 'aahs'.

He had provided himself with an unshakable alibi. At the time the robbery took place he was in the offices of the *People*, telling Duncan Webb the concluding part of his life story.

The first episode of 'The Amazing Confessions of Billy Hill' had appeared in the *People* on 8 September, two weeks before the robbery took place. This peculiar mixture of romantic fantasy and down-to-earth exposé, brutal fact and richly embellished fiction, was guaranteed to upset a lot of people on both sides of the law. On 15 October details were published on how the KLM robbery was carried out. Even with Hill's cast-iron alibi it was an extraordinary thing to do and it is unlikely that Hill would have been so open had he not planned to emigrate. In April 1955 he sailed, with Gypsy, to Australia. But for once, Hill had been too clever for his own good and he was caught by his own propaganda. The Australian authorities steadfastly refused to admit the 'Boss of Britain's Underworld', despite his protestations that he had now retired and wanted to live an honest life. In June he sailed back to Britain.

By this time relations between Spot and

A turning point: Billy Hill before the long voyage home from Australia.

Hill were deteriorating and Spot, left at home to mind the underworld, was facing increasingly serious problems. A new 'guv'nor' of the West End, Superintendent Herbert Sparks, was trying to make a name for himself by cleaning up Soho. He was helped by the Prevention of Crime Act of 1953, which made it an offence to carry any sort of weapon. In September 1953 Spot had been arrested for possession of a knuckleduster. He protested that as a protector of bookmakers it was essential for him to be armed, and he escaped with a £50 fine, but it was still a humiliating experience. As Sparks comments in his autobiography, *Iron Man*, 'to be pulled in, searched and then booked like some petty thief' was, for big men like Spot, 'an intolerable blow to their high opinion of themselves'. Returns from the racing business were being squeezed as the Jockey Club, encouraged by the big credit bookies, enforced more and more stringent controls in preparation for the expected legalization of off-course betting. With a smaller cake there was inevitable dissension about the share-out and Spot was finding his wishes and instructions continually thwarted by a group of Italian bookies led by Albert Dimes.

Spot took Hill's claim to be boss of the underworld as a calculated insult. Webb, whom he blamed for fostering Hill's delusions of grandeur, was summoned to the Horse-shoe pub in Tottenham Court Road, taken round the back and given a good hiding. Having successfully eluded attempts by the Messinas and their henchmen to beat him up, Webb was nonplussed to have his pipe knocked out of his mouth and his arm broken by Spot's knuckleduster. He complained to the police and Spot was arrested. Hill advised him that there were better ways of obtaining revenge and when Spot was brought to trial the charge was reduced and again he escaped with a £50 fine.

Spot's action was rash and stupid – an indication that he was slipping. Family life was making him unsuited for his role. In his highly coloured biography, *Jack Spot: The Man of a Thousand Cuts*, Hank Janson points out: 'Jack Spot, who was the Boss of the Underworld, was now living a Jekyll and Hyde existence. He was a happy, contentedly married man in his home, and a scheming, planning master-mind at his club.' An associate of Spot's put it more succinctly: 'What were the boys to think when the phone rang for Jack and he would tell us, "Sorry, boys, must go home, the baby's crying."' Getting involved in an unseemly brawl with a journalist hardly improved his image, and when Spot's own story appeared in the second-rate *Sunday Chronicle* (which was soon to close down), it seemed derivative and unimaginative compared to Hill's.

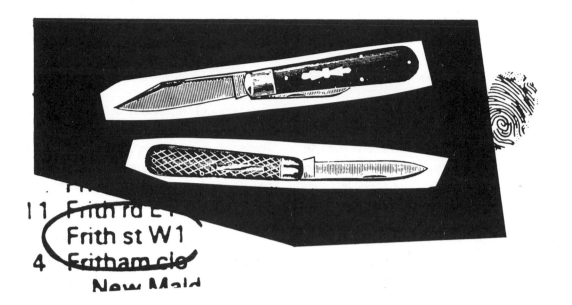

10 THE BATTLE OF FRITH STREET

I walked the streets, my brain quivering and as raw and as sensitive as a snail stripped of its shell. Dimes, Dimes! DIMES! The name hammered in my head, thundered in my blood and hissed through my veins. Without knowing it, I was approaching Soho, striding down Charlotte Street. I turned into Frith Street, where the morning shoppers crowded the pavements, bustled in and out of shops and stared at me strangely as I strode past with a wild look in my eyes. Dimes, Dimes! DIMES!

Hank Janson, *Jack Spot: The Man of a Thousand Cuts* (1959)

The fall of Jack Spot

By the middle of 1955 the Italian bookies were in open dispute with Spot. Hill had returned from Australia in time for the Derby and was seen at Epsom alongside Italian bookies and strong-arm men Albert Dimes, Pasquali Papa, Johnny Ricco and Tommy Falco. Spot recruited the young Kray twins in case of trouble. To their disappointment there wasn't any. Spot was anxious to avoid full-scale gang warfare, which would inevitably provoke a police crackdown, but he decided to make an example of Albert Dimes, a handsome, genial Italian who was currently employed as one of Hill's bodyguards (though, according to Spot, 'he couldn't bodyguard a flea'). The showdown occurred, rather ignominiously, in a Soho greengrocer's shop on 11 August. The *Daily Express* graphically sets the scene:

The hands of the clock above the Italian Expresso coffee bar pointed to 11.40. Mambo music was blaring from juke boxes. Men in slouched hats and draped suits were taking the air on the corner. Two men were talking under the clock . . . then as 50-year-old proprietor Mr Harry Hyams was weighing tomatoes the fight started inside his greengrocer's shop. A stiletto rose and ploughed swiftly as the two men fought. Trays of plump melons and plums and peaches toppled down as customers fled, and then 13 stone Mrs Sophie Hyams went into action. She picked up a heavy metal scoop from a weighing machine and began beating the fighting men over the head with it. The men tried to get out of the way. The stiletto kept flashing, but 45-year-old Mrs Hyams kept on banging the scoop at the men as the blood splashed on her white overall . . . Jack Spot staggered down the street alone as the juke boxes blared. He slumped into the scarlet and cream salon of a hairdressing shop. 'Fix me up,' he whispered. 'Clean me up,' said the man with a six-guinea shirt and £15 pair of shoes.

In fact the fight had started further up Frith Street when Spot had found Dimes hanging around outside the Bar Italia, engaged in his usual street-betting activities, and hit him on the chin. Down but not out, Dimes scrambled up and ran for his life into the Continental Fruit Store on the corner of Frith Street and Old Compton Street. The enraged Spot grabbed a small potato knife and stabbed Dimes a couple of times before he received a ringing blow on the head from Mrs Hyams. This gave Dimes the opportunity to fight back and he began stabbing wildly at his bemused opponent. In the end the two men, both bleeding profusely, staggered out into the street and separated. Dimes was helped into a taxi by Pasquali Papa (Bert Marsh) and driven off to hospital. Spot slid slowly to the pavement, where he sat for a few moments, bleeding from wounds in the face, arm, head and chest and with his fifty-guinea suit ripped and blood-stained. People hesitated to approach him, but he rose to his feet and stumbled into the Italian barber's a few doors away.

Spot's wounds healed quickly, but as he recovered in hospital his empire crumbled into dust. Duncan Webb gleefully celebrated the downfall of 'Jack Spot – the Tinpot Tyrant' in the *People* the following Sunday, and claimed that at last 'the mob had discovered what I had known for years – that Spot is a poseur who had got away with it by boasting'. While this was hardly unbiased reporting, in making a personal attack on Dimes, Spot had made a disastrous mistake. He had involved himself in an unseemly brawl, in full view of a shocked but inquisitive public with a man who, whatever his faults, was a popular local figure. Unlike the sallow, ulcer-ridden chiv-man Teddy Machin, who deserted Spot for Hill, Dimes was known and trusted by a large number of people. His advice was sought after in the settlement of disputes and he acted as unofficial banker to many imprisoned criminals. Dimes was the worst possible candidate Spot could have chosen to make an example of. In 1941 he had been involved in the murder of 'Little Hubby' Distelman but by the fifties Jewish/Italian conflicts had lost their political and communal dimension and become a matter of personal vendetta. (There is a certain irony that 'Italian Albert' Dimes should seek shelter in a Jewish fruiterer's while Spot's refuge was an Italian barber's shop.)

Both men made surprisingly rapid recoveries in view of the damage they had inflicted on each other. Spot (in Middlesex Hospital) had stab wounds in the left cheek, above the left eye, several in the left arm and two in the chest – one of which had penetrated the lung cavity. Dimes (in Charing Cross Hospital) had his forehead cleft open, minor lacerations of the chin and left thumb, a wound on the left thigh and one in the stomach (which was to cause him problems in later life). But within eleven days they were pronounced fit enough to stand trial and were summoned to Marlborough Street magistrate's court and charged jointly with causing an affray in a

The genial gangster: Albert Dimes with his wife.

public place, with possessing an offensive weapon and of causing grievous bodily harm. They pleaded not guilty (Dimes had complained indignantly to the police, 'Spottie does me up and I get pinched') and the case was transferred to the Old Bailey to begin on 19 September.

Events didn't turn out quite as the police had hoped. The judge, Mr Justice Glyn-Jones, was something of a stickler for the proper presentation of a charge and was unwilling to allow that a fight which took place mainly inside a private shop constituted an affray in a public place. He advised the jury to dismiss the charge and decided that on the other charges Spot and Dimes should be tried separately. This was to have unforeseen and dramatic consequences.

Spot's trial began on Thursday 22 September before the Recorder of London, Sir Gerald Dodson. At first everything seemed to go well for the prosecution. Mr and Mrs Hyams and their son Alec, and the Italian bookmakers Pasquali Papa (Bert Marsh) and Sebastian Boonacore, proved unshakeable in their testimony that Spot was the aggressor and that Dimes was merely defending himself. As his counsel Spot had appointed Rose Heilbron, a young barrister who would eventually become a High Court judge. She was Jewish and Spot hoped she would be sympathetic to his cause, but there was little she could do in what seemed to be an open and shut case. Spot himself proved a less than satisfactory witness, arguing not only that Dimes had attacked him but that, as he had never had possession of the knife, Dimes's injuries must have been self-inflicted. But towards the end of the afternoon, the defence was able to produce a witness who seemed to corroborate Spot's version of events.

Christopher Glinski, a Polish air officer whose exploits during the war had won him the Polish Military Cross and the French Croix de Guerre, claimed he had been in Frith Street and saw Spot push the other man.

Then the other man charged him. The other man took a knife out of his pocket. The man in the dock lifted his arms to defend himself. I saw the knife cut into his arm. Then I saw another blow cut his face. They got hold of one another and, together, staggered into the shop.

This tipped the balance in Spot's favour but it would have been unlikely to outweigh the evidence of the Hyams family and the Italian bookies. Men claiming brilliant war flying records who turned out to be spivs and murderers were not uncommon in the aftermath of the Second World War (most notably the murderers Neville Heath and Donald Hume). Glinski's war record was genuine enough but it would later emerge that he was a familiar figure among the Spot retinue. However, on the second (and final) day of the trial the defence produced, like a rabbit from a hat, a much more impressive witness in the form of an ancient clergyman, the eighty-eight-year-old Basil Claude Hudson Andrews.

The distinguished old gentleman claimed that he had read newspaper reports of the court proceedings and decided something was seriously wrong. 'It astonished me,' he claimed. 'I thought, "Dear me! This is entirely wrong! The *darker* man was the aggressor. He attacked the *fairer* man."' He then proceeded to identify Dimes as the darker man and Spot as the fairer man. 'At first I thought I had better keep quiet about it. But it preyed on my mind. Ultimately I decided I had better do something.' The parson's evidence had the desired effect and after sixty-five minutes' deliberation, the

Venerable perjurer: Parson Basil Andrews.

jury decided that Spot was not guilty. Amidst wild cheering, 'reminiscent of the winning of a heavyweight boxing championship', the Recorder ordered Spot to be released – though not before admonishing him to behave himself as he danced up and down in the dock, hands clasped above his head.

Parson Andrews had asked the Recorder if his name could be kept out of the papers, commenting, 'I am pretty well known in London and have groups of friends, and it is rather a disgraceful affair to be mixed up in.' It was soon to be revealed who those 'groups of friends' were. Albert Dimes had only been present in court for identification purposes, and there is little doubt that had he appeared as co-defendant with Spot he would have instructed his counsel to question Parson Andrews about his background. Instead he passed on a few useful items of information to Duncan Webb.

Webb had not been present in court, but he soon got busy – talking to several Soho bookies and chatting up the maid at the parson's Paddington lodgings. By Saturday night he had a story, and splashed across the front page of later editions of the *People* on Sunday was the headline: 'Parson's Dud Bets Start Hunt by Bookies.'

The perjury trials

Webb reported that three bookies recognized Andrews as someone they knew very well as the 'knocking Parson'. According to one of them, 'He opened an account with me and on his first day's betting lost £35. We haven't

seen him since. A few days later he had laid bets with another West End bookmaker. He lost £15 10s and was not heard of again.' Parson Andrews had been curate at Kensal Green cemetery for thirty-nine years, retiring in 1947 on a pension of £250 a year. However, his career in the church seemed to have been severely hampered by a weakness for whisky, women and gambling, and since retirement he had established a reputation among Soho bookies for not paying his often substantial gambling debts. He was also well practised in the art of 'telling the tale' – reciting mournful hard-luck stories to elicit the sympathy and money of soft-hearted benefactors.

The parson was now big news and the *Daily Sketch* decided it would be worthwhile to take him under their wing. He was spirited away to a hotel where he would be safe from the prying pens of other journalists and asked to dictate a letter which would disperse the cloud of suspicion about the veracity of his evidence. It was published on Monday 26 September and – like the parson's evidence at the trial – appeared sincerely convincing. After complaining about 'cowardly people who dare not come forward into the light of day' and their base suggestions that he had lied to the court, he went on:

I would recall to you that when I gave evidence last week I gave it on my solemn oath, and I need not remind you that I am a Clerk in Holy Orders also. I therefore wish to affirm in the most solemn terms that what I said in the witness-box was the whole truth and nothing but the truth. I wish to deny that I have committed perjury. I wish to deny that I have any hopes of material gain from having come forward as a witness. I did so only in the interests of truth, and I am willing to tell the police that if they come to me. Any financial difficulties due to my change of address and my harmless flutters in the sporting world are only temporary, due to my age and inexperience.

He concluded with a suitably sanctimonious desire 'to bring about a reconciliation between the parties in strife who seem to have forgotten that, by what they have done, they are debasing the sacred Brotherhood of Man'. But the Brotherhood of Man had not yet finished with Parson Andrews.

At the trial of Albert Dimes, held that same Monday, the prosecution conceded that, in view of the outcome of the Spot trial and the events of the weekend, it would be unsafe to convict Dimes, and Sir Gerald Dodson directed the jury to return a formal verdict of not guilty. With both men acquitted, the police had to contend with derisive comments about 'the fight that never was'. But they were determined not to let the matter rest. An investigation was launched under Chief Superintendent Edward Greeno, the Met's top CID officer. Greeno's right-hand man, Superintendent Herbert Sparks, had been appointed head of C Division (West End Central) in 1953 and hailed as the 'Iron Man' who would clean up Soho. Now his reputation was looking a little tarnished and both men were determined to prevent Spot making any sort of come-back. Before long they had induced the aged parson to reveal a remarkable conspiracy.

While tottering around the lobby of the Cumberland Hotel at Marble Arch on 14 September, penniless and in need of someone to buy his breakfast. Parson Andrews had been approached by Peter MacDonough, a small-time gambler and friend of Jack Spot. MacDonough had rented rooms to the parson a year earlier and had a soft spot for the old rogue. He was struck by the thought that he could do both Spot and the parson a favour, and told him 'You can earn some money if you would care to say six words.' Naturally the hungry parson was interested and he was soon introduced to Moisha Blueball (Morris Goldstein) and Sonny the Yank (Bernard Schach), two of Spot's long-standing henchmen who were sticking with him when most Spot followers were disappearing into the undergrowth. He was taken round to the Spots' Hyde Park Mansions flat, introduced to Rita and given a cup of tea and a tale to tell Bernard Perkoff, the Spot solicitor. All he had to say was that he had been in Frith Street on 11 August, seen the fight and was certain that it was Dimes who had attacked Spot and not the other way round. Over the next few days he was given a total of £63 (it should have been £65 but Moisha couldn't resist cheating him of a couple of pounds). He was also told that he 'would never want' and that 'he'd always be provided for' if Jack was acquitted – though, in view of the way in which he was bustled away from Spot's celebration party after the trial, such promises didn't amount to much.

With the parson's story, and some slight but useful corroborative evidence from the commissionaire at the Cumberland Hotel and a resident of Hyde Park Mansions, the police felt ready to prosecute the conspirators. Early in October Moisha, Sonny and MacDonough

Spot's henchmen, Morris Goldstein (Moisha Blueball) and Bernard Schach, known as Sonny the Yank.

were arrested and two weeks later Rita Comer was brought back from Ireland, where she and Spot had retreated to avoid unwelcome publicity. Their trial began on 28 November before Mr Justice Ormerod.

Behind their massed ranks of lawyers (two for each of the four defendants), Rita, Mac-Donough, Moisha and Sonny were confident that the case against them would founder on the problem of using a self-confessed and possibly senile perjuror as the chief witness against them. In fact Parson Andrews put up an even more impressive performance than he had done at the Spot trial. The dubious events of his past life were mercilessly dredged up and subjected to courtroom scrutiny. But with a combination of pathos and toughness, roguery and genuine repentance, he stood up to it all very well. He admitted that he had 'borrowed money from many people and failed to pay it back' and that he had been guilty of many shady things in his past (though he added pointedly, 'Isn't everybody?'). His tone of pathetic eloquence proved very effective. Asked why he had lied at the Spot trial, he replied:

It was very wicked of me. I was very hard up and I was tempted and I fell. It is rather humiliating for me to have to tell you I was desperately hungry. I had had what is called Continental breakfasts and nothing in between. I was very poor and hungry and I should not have yielded but I did. Thank God, I have asked to be forgiven!

Pressed to explain why he had now decided to tell the truth, the old man told the hushed court, 'In the silence of the night, when things come back to you, it was brought to my mind the sin I had committed and the wickedness I had done and the harm I had caused by acting as I had done.'

But the parson was by no means abject in his shame for his misdeeds, and pathos was intermixed with a healthy dose of anger, indignation and wit. When accused by Moisha's QC, David Weitzman, of being an incorrigible liar, he protested:

I have not come here to tell lies. I have come here to try to undo the lies I did tell at the trial. Your object is to damn me. I was determined then and there, not because I was influenced by any individual, to tell the truth at all costs, although I should have to confess to the public that I had been a most dreadful liar. But I have done it, and I am very glad I have. I feel much happier about it.

He became increasingly impatient with Weitzman's claim that he had invented the whole conspiracy and retorted, 'Oh, I must have dreamt it, mustn't I?' And when Weitzman persisted with his line of argument, burst out with, 'All this sounds to me like a fairy story.'

With nothing to lose in this unexpected epilogue to his very long life, Andrews gave a remarkable performance, cleverly using his deafness and fading memory to defeat the sarcasm of his persecutors. Even the wittiest lines tend to backfire when they have to be repeated over and over again, and after seven and a half hours in the witness box the parson was still uncowed, politely requesting the defence lawyers to repeat their questions a little louder, stubbornly insisting that despite his earlier lapse he was not an untruthful man.

In summing up, Mr Justice Ormerod warned of the dangers of convicting on the testimony of someone who had not only been involved in the conspiracy but had admitted to lying under oath. Such evidence, however, could be accepted if it was corroborated from other sources, or if the jury was convinced that the witness was telling the truth and had no motive for lying, as in the case of Parson Andrews. The corroborative evidence, particularly the self-incriminatory 'verbals' attributed by the police to Moisha, Sonny, Rita and MacDonough when they were arrested, was extremely weak and it was the persuasive testimony of Parson Andrews which swayed the jury in finding the conspirators guilty. Moisha Blueball was sent down for two years – his first prison sentence. Sonny the Yank and Peter MacDonough were given a year. Rita, a model young mum, with her two pretty little daughters, her Irish charm and her devotion to her husband, received only a six-month suspended sentence and a £50 fine.

The Parson Andrews conspiracy trial comes across as a comic pre-echo of the supergrass trials of the seventies and eighties. And if most of the limelight fell on the eighty-eight-year-old clergyman, the defendants contributed lively cameo performances. Moisha Blueball (changed to 'Blueboy' so as not to offend the public's sensibilities, though the nickname came from the delicate state of one of his testicles), came across as a sharp but sentimental Jewish 'wide boy'. He challenged the statements attributed to him by pointing out that his persecution complex would prevent him from using words like 'schtum' when talking to Gentiles – particularly when they were policemen. Sonny the Yank, who told the court he was a 'donkey greaser' from Stepney, demonstrated how his false teeth fell out when he became excited and protested that he was only at Hyde Park Mansions under the Old Pals Act. Rita, looking for all the world like Margaret Lockwood in her Wicked Lady roles, played the loyal devoted wife sufficiently well to save herself from a custodial sentence.

The trial of Christopher Glinski, the Polish air officer, was a much less entertaining affair, but it raised very serious issues. Glinski had been arrested for perjury in October and was brought for trial before Mr Justice Ormerod on 7 December. As there was no way of proving that he had not been present at Frith Street or that his interpretation of what had happened was not a plausible one, the only chance of securing a perjury conviction was to prove that he had lied about never having seen Spot before, and lied about never having been to the Hyde Park Mansions flat. Again the parson was wheeled on, this time to say he had seen Glinski at the Spot flat, but he admitted he hadn't actually spoken to him and it was not too difficult for Glinski's counsel, the Conservative MP William Rees-Davies, to cast doubt on the clergyman's ability to recall faces and events accu-

rately. Mrs Smyth, a neighbour of Spot, also claimed to have seen Glinski, but her evidence was too vague to be conclusive.

However, the case for the prosecution didn't rest solely on the flimsy testimony of these two witnesses. Glinski's 'verbals', the remarks he allegedly made when he was arrested, seemed to condemn him out of his own mouth. Chief Inspector John Manning, Sparks's second-in-command, reported that, on being arrested, Glinski told him:

Look, the trial is over. We had advice and now you can do nothing about it. I never talked about the evidence of the parson and nobody can prove that I did. If Hubby Distelman has been talking about me going to the flat, I will do him. It must be him because he is the only one who knows about me going to Comer's flat. Moisha and Sonny won't squeal, and Mrs Comer isn't there. I will still beat you.

Glinski vigorously denied that he said anything like this, and Rees-Davies, pointing out that it added up to 'a miracle of admission', questioned whether such language wasn't more appropriate to 'one of the thugs of the East End' than to a middle-class Pole. Had the police been able to produce 'Big Hubby' Distelman their case would have been much stronger. Distelman, who for over twenty years had prospered as a police informer, undoubtedly knew about the conspiracies hatched at Hyde Park Mansions. But in this case he wasn't prepared to help. Fourteen years earlier Albert Dimes had helped to murder his brother.

In all probability Glinski was as guilty as the parson in claiming to have seen what happened in Frith Street, though his interpretation of events is probably closer to the truth than that of the Hyams family and the Italian bookies. But Rees-Davies managed to shift the emphasis away from whether or not Glinski had been at the Spot flat to the accuracy or otherwise of what he was supposed to have said to the police. It was a dangerous move, as juries generally accepted that the police were unimpeachably honest. As Mr Justice Ormerod pointed out in his summing up:

There is no mincing of words in this case. The attitude of the defence is that those two police officers [Sparks and Manning] invented this conversation, that it is a tissue of lies from beginning to end. They say that not one word was ever said by Glinski and that it is sheer imagination and put in by the police officers for the purpose of bolstering up the evidence of Andrews and Mrs Smyth. It is not suggested, as it is sometimes, that the police have been mistaken in hearing what was said or that the recollection of the police is at fault. It is suggested that the police officers were deliberately lying when they gave their evidence.

In his autobiography, *Iron Man*, published in 1964, Superintendent Herbert Sparks remarks, 'It doesn't matter how viciously or cleverly a policeman is cross-examined in the witness-box, how often he may be tripped up and made to look a fool – if he is telling the truth the jury will seldom be confused.' It was something of a blow to his credibility, then, that after deliberating for fifty minutes, the jury found Glinski not guilty.

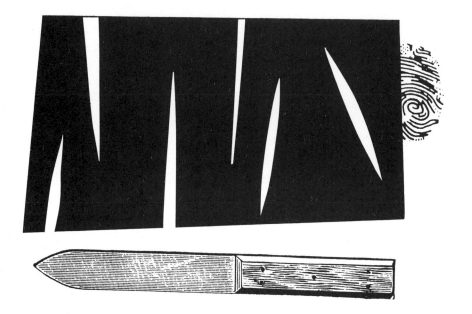

11 MAN OF A THOUSAND CUTS

No doubt the pimps and procurers are associated with the ruffians who pursue their beastly feuds with knife and pistol in the mean streets adjoining the West End. The financial basis of these people's nasty existence is bound to be something of a mystery to the law-abiding subject. It is seldom suggested that any of them has ever done a hand's turn of honest work; and statisticians who have studied such comparatively decent folk as burglars and pickpockets report that there is only a very jejune living to be made out of straightforward theft. Yet the gangsters travel in expensive motor cars, indulge in costly debauches, and wear purple and fine linen, which they can hardly acquire by preying upon one another.

The Times, 29 June 1956

Corruption in Soho

During the Greeno investigation and the Parson Andrews conspiracy trial there had been vague intimations of police corruption, and crooks had threatened to 'blow the top' about police methods in the West End. Rees-Davies had felt able to make his frontal assault on the integrity of Superintendent Sparks because the police were already in trouble. In November 1955 Duncan Webb had warned:

At the root of the canker of corruption that is steadily getting its grip on London is a growing network of late-night drinking clubs that are the source of vice in all its form. These unsavoury places are controlled by a handful of operators – many of them with police convictions. The power these men exercise over others is so great that they are now virtually the bosses of the underworld. They corrupt girls by selling them into vice, the 'business' of which they control. They corrupt men into criminals and drug addicts – and they are even prepared to corrupt the police.

Another trial at the Old Bailey held a few weeks before the Glinski trial revealed alarming facts about the extent of police corruption in Soho and the West End.

Joseph Grech was a Maltese pimp who, in partnership with Tony Micallef, a brother-in-law of the Messinas, had moved into the vacuum created by the enforced absence of the Messina brothers. In July 1954 he had been arrested on a house-breaking charge after a police search of his home turned up the key to a recently burgled flat. He was most indignant when he was found guilty and sent down for three years, and his persist-ent allegations that he had been framed by crooked policemen eventually resulted in an investigation by Detective Superintendent Herbert 'Suits' Hannam, a policeman who was something of a maverick in the drabbly dressed ranks of the CID. He had led the successful hunt for the Teddington Towpath murderer in 1953, and robustly rebutted defence claims that he had fabricated the confession of Alfred Whiteway, the alleged murderer. Hannam claimed to have uncovered a conspiracy involving solicitor Ben Canter, who had acted for the Messinas and had the biggest criminal practice in London; Morris 'Spider' Page, a contact man and go-between who thrived by arranging mutually useful meetings between policemen and criminals; and Sergeant Robert Robertson, an ex-member of the Ghost Squad, who for a number of years had worked with the Vice Squad at West End Central. They were brought for trial before Lord Goddard, the Lord Chief Justice, at the Old Bailey on 17 November 1955.

Grech's story was that, at the suggestion of 'Spider' Page, Robertson agreed to lend Grech the key to the burgled flat so that he could have a lock made in his own flat which the key would fit, thus offering a legitimate explanation for why it was found there. With the help of Canter and Page this was done, but Grech neglected to straighten Robertson's superior officer, Inspector Charles Reuben Jacobs – who wanted a minimum payment of £500 – and the irate Jacobs detailed two of his men to swear that they had seen Grech hanging around the burgled flat. This resulted in his conviction.

Grech's account seemed to be confirmed by the extremely detailed and damaging verbals Hannam had collected. As in the Spot perjury trials, they were vigorously denied by the defendants. But whether they were true or not, here they were much more convincingly presented. Canter, for example, on being asked to arrange a meeting with Tony Micallef, apparently told Hannam:

He won't tell you who the locksmith was that altered the lock. I can't tell you either. How can I? If I did I would be in it as well. You know what is sometimes done in a defence. I thought it would work the oracle and get him off. Don't hold it against Jock Robertson. He is a decent bloke and he only loaned us the key – Spider fixed the rest.

While Page told him that Grech didn't do the burglary himself 'but he had the monkey out of the peter and some groins, but they were tripe'.

Crime reporter Laurence Wilkinson expressed scepticism about Hannam's ability to recall accurately, without the aid of notes, long and convoluted interviews verbatim, but he was impressed by their seeming authenticity. Leonard 'Nipper' Read, the man who brought the Krays to justice, worked with Hannam in the fifties and claimed he had a photographic memory:

He was actually able to recite pages and pages of statements, and he taught me to do it as well. It wasn't a question of being selective: you wrote down what you remembered and Hannam was brilliant at this.

There was no question here of inserting a couple of Yiddish words because the suspect was Jewish, or of Polish air officers speaking like East End thugs. Canter, Page and Robertson may not have said what Hannam said they said, but they seemed to be the sort of thing they would say. And there remained the possibility that they were true. Questioning how incriminatory statements could have been extracted from a solicitor as astute as Canter, Wilkinson surmised:

One possible answer to that question carries with it a grave implication. It is that Canter could have been accustomed to making statements to police officers 'off the record', in the confident belief that they would not be repeated where they ought to be repeated – in court. Other evidence might seem to reinforce this deduction. There was his invitation to 'please forget it'. There was his claim that 'Some police officers are co-operative.'

The jury found them guilty of conspiracy to pervert the course of public justice. Canter was sentenced to two years' imprisonment. Page to fifteen months, Robertson to two years and he was dismissed from the Force. It did Grech, the chief prosecution witness, little good. Lord Goddard saw no reason to overturn the verdict the jury had come to at his trial and the disgruntled pimp was sent back to complete his sentence.

Sergeant Robertson, like Sergeant Goddard in the twenties, might have been written off as a bad apple in an otherwise incorruptible police force had not Grech's allegations gone much further and been backed up – indeed amplified – by Superintendent Hannam. His confidential report to the Commissioner of the Metropolitan Police, Sir John Nott-Bower, was leaked to *Daily Mail* crime reporter Arthur Tietjen and, to the embarrassment of the police and the government, it was splashed over the front page on the day the trial opened. It made sensational reading. According to Tietjen, Hannam, after interviewing more than forty men serving prison sentences and a number of police officers, discovered that:

Gaming houses, where faro and chemin-de-fer were being played quite openly, were tipped off at a 'fee' when a raid was to take place. Proprietors were warned to get 'mugs' in on a certain day, so that the regular customers could escape arrest. Brothel-keepers were told that certain evidence could be 'adjusted' at a price. Huge sums of money changed hands. The 'adjustment' was for an officer to say in evidence that upon the raid taking place he found a number of fully clothed women in the premises, whereas, in fact, they were nude. That gave the premises an air of respectability – and halved the fine.

Prostitutes too, were included in the bribery racket. Most of them were arrested on a regular basis and fined £2 for soliciting. According to Hannam, police officers were willing to postpone arrests and court appearances if they were paid an appropriate fee. And the 450-odd Soho basement clubs were tolerated because they contributed to unofficial police funds. 'The owners of these unsavoury clubs are usually "wide-boys" who would not otherwise get custom from their various associates. But no objection is raised by the police when prospective owners appear and ask for a form to sign to open a club.'

Hannam claimed that some uniformed policemen were receiving up to £60 a week in bribes (at a time when a police constable's wage was from £9 to £11 a week) and that

'protection' extended into the courts. Police officers habitually committed perjury: 'Evidence was "cooked" by police officers to benefit accused people. Details of previous convictions were suppressed in many instances, so that men standing on charges were fined nominal sums, instead of going to prison.'

Sir John Nott-Bower was flustered into denying that there was any such report. And he reassured the assembled officers of West End Central – the station at which malpractice was said to flourish – that the allegations of corruption were an unwarranted attack upon a fine and conscientious body of men and women and that there was no truth whatsoever in the rumour that 450 men were to be transferred from a Central London division. The *Daily Mail* conceded that Hannam hadn't actually recommended the transfer of 450 men. But in view of the Challenor affair, which was to erupt in 1963, and the endemic corruption surrounding the Drugs and Vice Squads in the sixties and seventies, it was a pity such sensible advice remained unheeded.

Boss of Britain's underworld

On 15 November 1955, two days before the Grech conspiracy trial opened, Billy Hill held a party at Gennaro's in Dean Street, Soho, to celebrate the publication of his autobiography, *Boss of Britain's Underworld*, ghost-written by Duncan Webb. With the exception of Jack Spot and his few remaining friends, all the leading figures of the underworld – Ruby Sparks, Eddie Chapman, Tommy Smithson, Teddy Machin – were there. Drifting among

them were ex-policemen like Chief Superintendent John Walsh and socialites like Lady
Docker. Still-active detectives like Sparks,
Greeno, Beveridge and Higgins kept well
clear. At a time when the underworld was
very much in the public eye both the party
and Hill's book attracted considerable media
attention. The *Daily Mail* reproduced the invitation sent to its reporter and concluded with
the comment: 'A sorry day, I feel, when a
gangster's book justifies a gilt-edged invitation.' 'William Hickey' in the *Daily Express*
thought these underworld celebrities 'sad
little men who have lost their way', though
he was diplomatic enough to describe Hill as
courteous and intelligent. The *Daily Sketch*
protested that Hill's book was a 'primer for

gangsters, hold-up men and cosh boys', full
of 'detailed instructions on the technique of
mayhem'.

Hitherto, criminal autobiographies had
been written by men saying a sometimes
regretful, sometimes relieved goodbye to their
criminal career. For all his protestations that
he had 'retired', Hill was still very much
involved in underworld life and he came
close to admitting that he had masterminded
two major unsolved crimes – the 1952 mailbag robbery and the 1954 KLM gold snatch.
Hill's insolent disrespect for the 'crime does
not pay' conventions of the criminal biography is to some extent masked by the book's
relentlessly unctuous sentimentality, but it
exposes parts of the underworld which had

Celebrating the publication of Billy Hill's autobiography, *Boss of London's Underworld*, at Gennaro's in
Soho (now the Groucho Club). Billy Hill is fourth from the left, and Ruby Sparks stands to his left.

never been explored before. It should not be mistaken for a straight factual account. Incidents that can be verified from other sources, such as the struggle for power between Jack Spot and the King's Cross Mob in 1946/7, are grossly distorted. But Hill's gutter-wise realism and Duncan Webb's hard-boiled romanticism combine fruitfully to give a startlingly vivid picture of the English underworld.

Much of Hill's story had already appeared in the *People* a year earlier, but its reappearance in book form coincided with the media's attempt to explain the goings-on of the underworld. The *Sunday Graphic*, opening a 'Casebook on Crime', commented: 'London is much the same as New York – the only real difference being that our laws of libel have curtailed graft and gangsterism in a velvet hush.' Opinion was polarized between those who thought that lifting the curtain, disturbing the hush, was fascinating and amusing and those who thought it shocking and scandalous. Questions were raised in the House of Commons as to why such a gathering at Gennaro's had been allowed and rabid editorials called for drastic action. Worries were expressed that Soho was becoming a fiefdom ruled by underworld barons. The *Daily Sketch*, under the heading 'CLEAN THIS CESSPOOL!', proclaimed:

The jealous rats fighting it out in the streets and the alleys could, in a short time, make Soho a desert where no respectable citizen would risk his reputation or his personal safety . . . Club owners and others who have managed to live peacefully in the past are now confronted by demands for protection money. The iron vice of crime is tightening on Soho. This is the ugliest challenge that the police have had to meet for many years in London . . . The only way to meet it is to deal with every single rat, however obscure he may appear at the moment. This is a job of vermin extermination.

In fact Soho had held a highly popular fair a few weeks before the Battle of Frith Street and for the young bohemians of the fifties the area held an irresistible appeal. George Melly thought it was 'the only area in London where the rules didn't apply . . . where bad behaviour was cherished – at any rate in retrospect – and only bores were made unwelcome'. That bookies and prostitutes, ponces and tearaways, thronged the narrow streets only added to the colour and excitement.

Newspapers sensed that their readers wanted to enjoy as well as condemn the activities perpetrated in London's 'square mile of sin'. Articles appeared attempting to explain to a bemused public how the English underworld operated. There were various reports of meetings held among London's gang chiefs to elect someone to the 'Empty Throne in Gangland'. The *News Chronicle* ran a three-day investigation of London's underworld, and the *Sunday Graphic* sent its reporter Norman Price to lunch with Ruby Sparks to find out if he was to become 'the new guv'nor'. Sparks told him a mob had been round and put the idea to him, but that he had cautiously declined to get involved. Most crime reporters were not very well equipped to sort out fact from fantasy when dealing with the underworld. Relations between the police and the press had improved markedly since the appointment of Sir Harold Scott as Commissioner of the Metropolitan

Police in 1945. And whenever one of Scotland Yard's 'big five' was sent out on an important murder case he would be accompanied by a loyal retinue of specialist reporters. They could expect to be kept informed of all the new developments as they came up, and in return were expected to show deference and respect to the wishes of the detective in charge of the case. Such methods of reporting were of little use in penetrating the underworld, where a much more sceptical attitude towards the police was required. Some reporters, like Laurence Wilkinson and Arthur Tietjen, were more realistic than their colleagues about the nature of the police, but they made no claim to any close contact with the underworld.

Reporters on popular Sunday newspapers like the *People*, *Sunday Chronicle*, *News of the World*, *Sunday Graphic* and *Empire News*, which often ran stories about famous crooks, were better placed to explain to the public the meaning of these violent stirrings in Soho. With the underworld polarized into opposing camps, however, crime correspondents found themselves getting deeply embroiled in its politics, having to take sides and report events from a biased point of view, which could involve them in dangerous situations. Webb, who visited Hill in Tangier during *The Flamingo* affair and wrote eulogies about him, had his wrist broken trying to ward off Jack Spot's knuckleduster. Gerald Byrne of the *Sunday Chronicle* was equally biased in favour of Jack Spot. He repeated judicial comments about Hill being 'a miserable little character' and ran stories on how he poisoned the pigeons of Trafalgar Square and put green ink in the fountains. Byrne's black Morris saloon was systematically wrecked shortly afterwards.

Hill was never one to shirk violent methods if peaceful ones failed, but part of his success must be reckoned his instinctive flair for public relations. Jack Spot and Albert Dimes both appeared on television and were made to look foolish protesting their innocence. Hill, his life moulded by the seventeen years he had spent inside, was uncompromisingly and unapologetically a criminal. ITN refused to show the interview they recorded with him and Granada abandoned the series of crime programmes they had planned to make with Duncan Webb when he insisted he should be allowed to interview Hill. Hill was too intelligent to be ridiculed and never safe enough to become a media personality.

Man of a thousand cuts

On a warm night early in May, Spot and his wife were strolling back from the Marble Arch Pavilion to their flat in Hyde Park Mansions. Within sight of their home they were surrounded by a large group of men carrying an assortment of weapons – razors, knives, coshes, even a shillelagh. Sensing what was about to happen, Rita screamed and Spot tried to get her up the steps leading to the flats. Halfway up they were caught. Rita clung tightly to her husband and refused to be parted from him. Together they were knocked to the ground and each of the men in turn aimed a blow at the ex-king of the underworld.

Seventy-eight stitches and a blood transfusion later, the battered, puffed eyes of Jack

Rita takes the lead: Mrs Comer precedes her husband into the courtroom
where she will name his attackers.

Spot, 'the King of Soho', blinked beneath a turban of bandages in St Mary's Hospital, Paddington. Outraged at the callousness of the attack and the indignity suffered by his wife, he agreed to name some of the men involved. But a week later he had retracted and was telling the press, 'I'm the toughest man in the world. I am staying in London. Nobody will ever drive me out.' But if Spot felt bound by the underworld code by which

he had lived his life, his wife felt no such inhibition. Rita, a tough Dublin girl, unimpressed by the ethos of the English underworld, persisted, despite threats and abuse, in naming several of the attackers.

On 5 May Bobbie Warren was arrested. Warren was closely associated with the Whites and his brother had been beaten up by Spot in 1947. On 14 May Frankie Fraser was arrested. Fraser was an up-and-coming south London tearaway but as a friend of the airport robber Georgie Woods, who had remained neutral throughout the Spot–Hill feud, he would be unlikely to bear any grudge against Spot. However, he was the sort of violent and unpredictable villain the police liked to keep safely locked up. Billy Hill, whom Rita insisted participated in the attack, was held for seven hours at Paddington police station but his alibi proved unshakeable. Warren and Fraser were picked out by Rita in an identification parade and brought before Mr Justice Donovan at the Old Bailey on 9 June.

Hill arranged for an Irish barrister, Patrick Marrinan, to represent his men. Marrinan, the son of a Royal Irish Constabulary officer turned barrister, had studied law at Queens University and had become a well-known figure in Belfast clubs and greyhound racing tracks. A keen boxer, he became heavyweight champion of the Irish Universities. In 1942 he had been convicted and fined for harbouring uncustomed goods in Liverpool. This setback meant that he was not called to the bar until 1951, but as a flamboyant and forceful barrister he rapidly made progress. By 1955 he was on very friendly terms with Billy Hill, and Hill arranged for him to move into a luxury flat in Seaforth Lodge, Barnes, where Hill himself lived.

In contrast to Duncan Webb, who was totally uninterested in material wealth, Marrinan was greedy, ambitious and unscrupulous. The involvement of such a venal character with leading figures in the underworld had disastrous consequences for Hill's men and eventually for Marrinan himself. The case against Warren and Fraser was not a strong one. The only evidence against them was Rita's insistence that they were among the attackers – and this was flatly contradicted by the evidence of her husband, who pointed to the dock and told the jury, 'I know these men never attacked me.' Asked to explain his statement naming Hill, Dimes, Warren, Falco and Fraser as among those who attacked him, he mumbled, 'I did not know what I was saying.'

A subtle barrister might have persuaded a jury that it was impossible to convict on such flimsy evidence, but Marrinan scored a series of own goals. Trying to clear Hill and Dimes from involvement in the attack, Marrinan provoked Superintendent McIver into responding that although he had initially been satisfied that neither man had been present, now he wasn't quite so sure. A Brighton bookmaker was produced to substantiate Fraser's claim that he had been nowhere near Hyde Park Mansions on the night of 2 May. But the police were allowed to reveal that he had three previous convictions – as a suspected person, for being on enclosed premises for an unlawful purpose and for attempting to steal six women's coats – and thus was not someone the court should believe unquestioningly. Marrinan's biggest blunder, though, was in his treatment of Rita.

His attempts to blacken Rita's character – revealing that she had lived with Spot before they married, stressing her involvement in the perjury conspiracy, accusing her of lying – only aroused sympathy for her. His attempt to expose her mercenary instincts by asking her to explain why she sold her picture to

Patrick Marrinan taking his daughter to school before a hard day in the courts
defending members of Billy Hill's entourage.

the *Daily Express* backfired when the judge commented ruefully, 'I wish they would pay me £300 for my photograph.' Marrinan's effort to portray her as a ruthless 'Queen of the Underworld' was disastrously misconceived. When he asked her, 'Is it not the truth that you are most anxious your husband should become the underworld king again?' she retorted tartly: 'I would be happy if my husband could be left alone and get just a small job. I have had enough of all this.' Neat, demure, determined, Rita was more than a match for this blustering bully.

In summing up, the judge pointed out that Rita had little to gain from making false accusations: 'If that story was false, what repercussions has she got to expect in this world of violence in which she and her children have been living for some time and which she told us she would give anything to escape?' It took the jury under two hours to find the luckless Fraser and Warren guilty and they were each sentenced to seven years.

Billy Hill had established his headquarters at the Rex café opposite the Old Bailey during the trial. With his dark glasses and snap-brim hat, and his entourage of broad-shouldered, broken-nosed and razor-slashed followers, he caused flurries of anxiety. The Old Bailey was ringed with extra large City of London policemen and Mr Justice Donovan was provided with a police escort to ensure that he wasn't interfered with by marauding mobsters. The press, disturbed at the emergence from the underworld of such threatening figures, protested loudly. 'Cassandra' in the *Daily Mirror* complained:

These hoodlums who have never done a day's work, who were brought up in Borstals, who have criminal records that leave the ordinary citizens reeling with horror at their callous brutalities, turn up in vast shiny limousines outside the courts of justice to encourage 'their boys' when all too occasionally they land in the dock.

And, he asked, 'Where is the new broom that will sweep and mop up the blood off our streets? Where is the Home Secretary and the Commissioner of Police who will drive these rats back into the gaol where they belong?' Hill's attempts to flout the authority of the law were not paying rich dividends. At the end of June three more of his men, William Patrick 'Billy Boy' Blythe, Robert 'Battles' Rossi and William 'Ginger' Dennis, were arrested and charged with the attack on Spot.

Their trial opened on 8 October before Mr Justice Cassels, with Marrinan again representing the defendants. Marrinan had already caused something of a stir by going over to Ireland to try to prevent the extradition of Blythe and Rossi. They had been brought back vigorously protesting their innocence and refused to take part in an identification parade. It did them little good. Rita confirmed that they were participants in the attack after being shown them in the Paddington Green police cells. Blythe might well have been innocent, but he was an associate of the King's Cross gang and the Clerkenwell Italians, and since he had slashed a policeman across the face in 1945 he had been a marked man. Running off to Ireland and staying in a house rented by Billy Hill when hitherto he'd never been further afield than

Southend hardly helped his case. On 16 October the three were found guilty. Blythe, who was sentenced to five years, was dragged away shouting, 'It's a mockery of justice.' Rossi and Dennis, who also protested their innocence, were each sentenced to four years.

Between the two trials of men accused of the attack on Spot and his wife, two other gangland trials became headline news. Frankie Fraser had been accused, along with Raymond Rosa and Richard Frett (also known as Dickie Dodo), of being among a group of men who had attacked Johnnie Carter, a Peckham fruit trader and aspiring south London gang leader, on 15 April. The attack was startlingly similar to the one made on Spot, except that they had broken down the door of the house in which Carter and his wife were sheltering before beating him with hammers, coshes, knives and shille-laghs; and rumour has it that the same south London gang was responsible for both jobs.

Only Frett and Rosa were brought for trial and they had the misfortune to come up before Mr Justice Donovan and to be represented by Patrick Marrinan. Carter and his wife had identified some of their attackers but at the trial they both refused to confirm their statements. The judge fulminated against the state of society when witnesses appeared to be too frightened to tell the truth and the jury found the two men guilty. Like Fraser and Warren, they were sentenced to seven-year prison terms. And if the jury had any qualms about sending men to long terms of imprisonment on insubstantial evidence, they were no doubt reassured when Frett

and Rosa's previous convictions were read out. Frett's eight offences included slashing an argumentative motorist across the face; Rosa's eight included slashing a man about the face and body after finding him in bed with his wife.

In summing up, Mr Justice Donovan complained that these sort of events were more appropriate to 'Chicago in the worst days of Prohibition than London in 1956'. It made an excellent headline when news filtered in that Tommy Falco had had his arm slashed outside the Astor Club near Berkeley Square and needed forty-seven stitches.

The Falco slashing

Falco claimed that he had been attacked by Jack Spot and he was backed up by his companion Johnny Rice (Ricco). As with the Frith Street incident, Spot looked irredeemably guilty and set for the same sort of sentence meted out to the men who had, a few weeks earlier, attacked him. Predictably he claimed he was entirely innocent and told the arresting policemen: 'You see what they do for me. I should have named the twenty of them.' And: 'This is a diabolical liberty. I will get ten years for nothing.' But there were a number of suspicious circumstances surrounding the case.

Because of threats to Rita and the children, Spot's flat had been under police observation. Admittedly it was intermittent observation, but Spot would still run the risk of being seen by a police patrol on leaving and entering his home; and after seeing Fraser and Warren sent down for seven years, it seemed

Tommy 'Bonz' Falco and Victor 'Scarface Jock' Russo.

improbable that he would endanger his freedom for the sake of a slash at Tommy Falco's
arm. There was also the odd fact that it
wasn't until nine hours after the attack that
Falco and Rice told the police that Spot was
the perpetrator.

Such puzzling factors might be put down
to the strange ways in which the underworld
carried on its vendettas; but as with the
Battle of Frith Street, Spot was rescued by a
deus ex machina, this time in the unlikely
guise of a diminutive Glasgow gangster,
Victor 'Scarface Jock' Russo. 'Cassandra' in
the *Daily Mirror* described him as 'a hacked-
up rat', 'a mutilated gorilla' and 'a degener-
ate with treachery in his heart, compared
with whom Judas was a thousandfold saint

who had the decency to find a tree and a
rope'. This was unfair, as with complete disre-
gard for his own safety he exposed a peculiar
plot.

Russo had come down from Scotland for
the racing at Epsom on 13 June. While he was
wandering around Soho on the following
Saturday, Johnny Rice, Tommy Falco, Albert
Dimes, Billy Hill and Franny Daniels drove
up alongside him in their big Buick. When
he got in the car, Dimes asked him, 'How
would you like another scar?' Apparently
Hill was infuriated at the heavy sentences
imposed on his men and wanted someone to
'take a stripe from Spot' (i.e. to be slashed by
one of Hill's men and to say he had been
attacked by Spot). As Russo's face was al-

ready criss-crossed with scars, it was thought one more wouldn't make much difference. Hill was prepared to offer a monkey (£500) before and another one after the job had been done. Russo protested that it would never work, but as Hill insisted he had everything set up, he accepted the money and, with the recklessness which was no doubt responsible for so many of his scars, returned to Glasgow and phoned Hill with the message: 'Thanks for the monkey, you dirty rat. If you ever come to Glasgow we'll send your body back in a sack!' Hill was thus left in something of a dilemma, and Falco, the least bright of his henchmen (in court he admitted he couldn't read much and asked Spot's counsel to 'use less big words'), was selected to play the absent Russo's role.

'Scarface Jock' was not the most reputable of witnesses – and there was the lurking memory that Spot had been acquitted before because of perjured evidence – but the prosecution was rattled enough to call on Hill and Dimes to rebut his story. Hill was as imperturbable as ever, lounging in the witness-box and peppering his answers with underworld jargon until rebuked by the judge (Mr Justice Streatfield). After Hill denied that he styled himself 'King of Soho', Spot's counsel asked him, 'What title do you take for yourself if not a kingdom or a dukedom?' He replied with perfect composure: 'The Boss of the Underworld'. Although he had been castigated as 'a miserable little character', it was evident to everyone in the courtroom that here was someone who was self-assured and powerful, and sufficiently contemptuous of the English legal system to organize just such

an outrageous conspiracy as Russo had described.

Nothing of Russo's past history emerged in the courtroom, both defence and prosecution being apprehensive of what might turn up. He was a cousin of Albert Dimes but there seems to have been little love lost between the two men. He had known Hill since 1940, but Russo – no mean practitioner with a knife himself – had slashed Hill's brother Archie on an earlier visit to London when he had attempted to disrupt his wooing of a pretty blonde club girl known as 'Manchester Maisie'. And on more than one occasion Spot had lent him money to get him out of a fix. On the other hand, he didn't seem the sort of character to invent an elaborate conspiracy and Spot no longer had any friends to put him up to it. Victor Durand, Spot's counsel, carefully trying not to put too much emphasis on his testimony, described Russo as a man 'without a bit of character', but he went on:

Perhaps I am being a bit unfair. Perhaps he has a little bit of character left in his backbone, a little bit of character which says at the last moment, 'I wouldn't do this.' Perhaps a tiny amount of pride, perhaps misplaced in such creatures, which says, 'I would not have it said afterwards that I put Comer away.'

Mr Justice Streatfield called Russo's account of the frame-up 'a strange story, one of the strangest that can ever have been told even in the Number One court of the Old Bailey'. But he was by no means prepared to dismiss it. Obviously something fishy was going on. Falco was not a normal habitué of the Astor Club and it seemed improbable

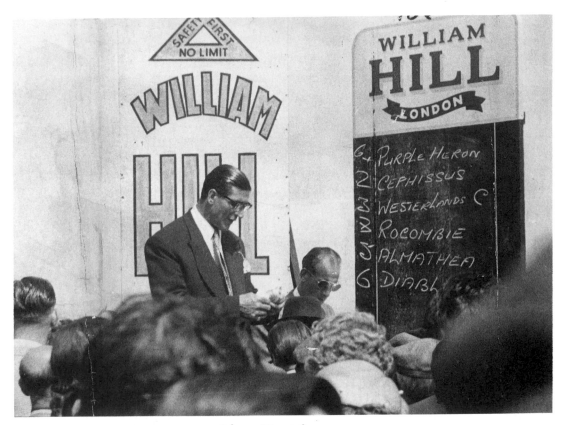

Johnny Rice at the races.

that Spot would run the gauntlet of the police watching his flat to lurk in the shadows of Mayfair on the off-chance of him appearing. Falco's wound, though not self-inflicted, was unusually straight and clean for a gangland slashing. And did Falco and Rice delay telling the police for fear that Spot would be found where he said he had been all night – at home in bed with his wife? Rita had made a bargain with God that her two little daughters would be baptized into the Catholic church if her husband was acquitted. Her prayers were answered. The jury took only twenty minutes to find Spot not guilty. There

were calls for Hill and his men to be prosecuted for perjury, but the prospect of relying on 'Scarface Jock' as the chief prosecution witness discouraged any further action.

Hill had planned to retire on publication of his story in the *People*, but the failure of his attempt to emigrate and the unrest which led to the fall of Jack Spot conspired to prolong his reign. Questions were asked in Parliament about Hill and his contempt for the law, and a spate of newspaper articles appeared explaining what exactly a 'Boss of the Underworld' did, and what qualifications were needed for the post. Most of them didn't

Tommy Smithson's losing hand: RIP, June 1956.

get further than Edgar Wallace-like tales of criminal masterminds. But a *Daily Herald* reporter perceptively pointed out:

Crime – even the shady rackets and 'concessions' which do not qualify for that title – does not pay to be disorganized. Gamblers want to run their dens without interference from ambitious 'gate-crashers'. So do the drinking-club operators, the bookies and the smaller fry. Remember – they can't go running to the police for protection. Hence the Boss. He must be an organizer, must possess brains which in the respectable world of business would win him a high place. And he must be ruthless enough to dispense a rough justice throughout the underworld. He is the underworld's distorted symbol of the respectable morality it defies. Quiet crime is his motto.

The *Herald* article, which appeared on 20 July, at the end of the Falco slashing trial, ended with a warning that the real menace came from the 'sex gangs of Soho'. Between the incident outside the Astor Club and the trial of Jack Spot another violent eruption had occurred. On 25 June Tommy Smithson was murdered in a Maida Vale brothel.

The Daily Sketch, trying to drum up opposition to Sydney Silverman's Death Penalty Abolition Bill, which was passing through Parliament, reported that the slaying was 'an almost exact copy of the movies'. 'It was carefully organized, it was done with efficiency and leisured speed. The killers had a car waiting with its engine running for the getaway.' But the fact that his killers were so quickly caught indicates that it was not quite the cold-blooded 'contract killing' the newspapers made out. Smithson had become such a nuisance to the Maltese ponces he was hired to protect that, in the underworld phrase, 'he had to go'. When arrested, Philip Ellul, a young Maltese ponce, admitted: 'Sure it was me that shot him, he was going to do me if I didn't get out of London and I don't stand for that.' But if the newspapers had invented a conspiracy where none existed, the murder was symptomatic, nevertheless, of a fragmentation of power within the underworld. Bernie Silver and Big Frank Mifsud had taken over from the Messinas as the leading vice racket operators and Smithson's violent end was an indication that 'quiet crime' was soon to be a nostalgic memory.

EPILOGUE

There were four of us in this firm, which was conducted in a very efficient way. Expenses had to be found to finance jobs, then when the jobs were done these were deducted from the total, and everyone was given his whack of whatever was left. It was just like a business – but illegal, that's all.

Peter Crookston, Villain (1967)

When Jack Spot was attacked and left bleeding in the gutter on the night of 2 May 1956 it marked the end of an era in the underworld as clearly as the Suez Canal crisis did in political life. Changes in the laws concerning gambling, prostitution and capital punishment were in the offing, and new gangs were growing up, contemptuous of the old order. In south London, the Richardsons, successful businessmen whose 'long firm frauds' brought them into increasingly violent contact with the underworld, were setting new parameters for crime. On the outer edges of east London, Big Jim Tibbs had taken over from the Upton Park mob and acknowledged allegiance to nobody. To cross the iron bridge into Canning Town, the western edge of Big Jim's fiefdom, was something even the boldest, fiercest and most ambitious of the new generation of gangsters – the Kray brothers – feared to do.

The Krays were the undisputed masters of the East End. They saw themselves as successors to Jack Spot and intended to follow him from the East End to the West:

We never had liked Spotty. We just turned out with him to show everyone that *we* was the up-and-coming firm and didn't give a fuck for anyone. Old Spotty understood. He knew quite well that though we were there in theory as his friends, we meant to end up taking over from him.

They had visited him in hospital after the gang attack and offered to organize revenge. He refused to discuss it and when they persisted he rolled over in his bed and turned away from them. Ronnie Kray had, nonetheless, paid a visit to the Italian Club in Clerken-

well and, with his heavy Mauser automatic, threatened Hill's allies. But without Spot's support a full gangland war was untenable.

Hill and the Krays and many other prominent underworld figures attended Tommy Smithson's funeral on 14 July 1956. Smithson, for all his limitations, was considered a 'game bastard' and worthy of respect. The funeral seemed to Hill an ideal opportunity for a *rapprochement* with the young East End leaders. Hill explained his intention of leaving England. He had bought a villa in Marbella and intended to retire to the sunshine to make up for the long years spent in damp prison cells. His wife, Aggie, would continue to run the New Cabinet Club in Gerrard Street and, though they were now estranged, he wished to ensure her well-being. He had interests in two other clubs and he intended to return to London occasionally to visit them. There was no longer any reason for conflict. The twins had the sense to agree.

Billy Hill enjoyed a period of prosperity and prestige in the sixties, maintaining his friendship with Lady Docker, gambling with Peter Rachman and Mandy Rice-Davis, making occasional appearances as an honoured guest at clubs run by the Kray brothers. He remained aloof and distant enough in his villa in Marbella to be untouched by the sixties gangland scandals. In the early seventies he returned to England and ran an up-market night-club in Sunningdale. His last years were, however, unhappy. In 1976 he split up with Gypsy and took up with a black singer. For a time they seemed deeply in love, a new emotion for the always inhibited Hill, but three years later she committed suicide. Hill became misanthropic and introspective and shut himself off from the world in his Moscow Road flat. He died in January 1984, 'the richest man in the graveyard', according to Spot.

Some of Hill's associates – notably Albert Dimes and Frankie Fraser – threw in their lot with the Richardsons. Dimes abandoned horse racing for a very lucrative racket supplying fruit machines to night-clubs. Frankie Fraser and Eddie Richardson joined him to make sure that nobody made any trouble. He became friendly with Stanley Baker and was introduced to the director Joseph Losey. It was Dimes who provided the authentic background detail which made Losey's 1960 film *The Criminal* (with Baker in the main part) so unusual among British crime films of the period. Dimes was not implicated in the fall of the Richardsons, but he never fully recovered his health from the Battle of Frith Street and he died in his River Street home in 1972, aged fifty-seven. Frankie Fraser was convicted as one of the Richardson 'torturers' in 1967 and his knack of upsetting prison warders meant that he served nineteen years inside. He was finally released in April 1985. Despite his fearsome reputation, I was assured that Fraser was 'the last man you would think of as a villain. Butter wouldn't melt in his bloody mouth.' This didn't prevent him from being gunned down outside Turnmills night-club, in the Farringdon area of London, in August 1991. Characteristically, he had nothing to say to the policemen waiting at his bedside.

Of other Hill associates, Little Billy Blythe died in prison after a 'stomach operation' in

Goodbye to another old friend: Billy Hill at Billy Blythe's funeral, February 1957.

February 1957, aged thirty-nine. Hill and other friends arranged a lavish funeral at Kensal Green cemetry, where Parson Andrews had spent so long as curate. Teddy Machin, the chiv-man whom Spot blamed for turning Hill against him, was severely wounded when two shotgun blasts were fired through the window of his home in Canning Town in 1970. Franny Daniels reached some sort of deal with the police in the seventies which made it imperative that he leave the country. He went to America where he had a nephew involved with the Mafia. Slip Sullivan proved as unlucky with his life as his rival Tommy Smithson. He had to serve twenty-one months for Hill's attack on Smithson in 1953, despite the fact that Smithson refused to testify. And then, in January 1955, he was stabbed in the ribs with a two-foot carving knife. Fears of gang warfare receded when rumours began to circulate that his assailant was his fiery Irish wife. She returned to Ireland when Sullivan died a week later and missed the spectacular funeral laid on by the underworld. Johnny Rice was sentenced to twelve months' imprisonment in May 1957 for receiving stolen car log books, obtaining books of petrol coupons by false pretences and stealing motor-cycle registration books. He refused to name anyone else involved in the racket – particularly not Billy Hill. Tommy Falco decided he had had enough of gangland after his arm healed and concentrated, with reasonable success, on his bookmaking activities. Eddie Chapman ran a successful night-club near Potter's Bar, north of London. But his refusal to act as an informer led to continual police raids and in the early seventies he made the commercially astute move of transforming the club into a health farm.

Both of Hill's earlier women prospered. Aggie had a slight setback when Selwyn Cooney, the manager of her New Cabinet Club in Gerrard Street, was murdered in February 1960 by Jimmy Nash, whose brother Johnny was aspiring to be the new boss of the underworld. In the seventies she moved to Jersey, where she opened a night-club and became a wealthy and respected member of the community. Gypsy was accused of stabbing out a man's eye at the Miramar Club, Paddington, in March 1957. But at the trial the one-eyed man, a Hammersmith coalman, said he had 'no idea' how he got his injury and the case was dismissed. Age softened even her tempestuous nature. Hill bought her a house in Ilford, and it was she who arranged his funeral and settled his affairs after his death.

Patrick Marrinan aroused the hostility of Chief Inspector Tommy Butler, later head of the Flying Squad, and an inquiry was held into Marrinan's dealings with Hill. Transcripts of their telephone conversations were passed over to the Bar Council and in June 1957 the Benchers of Lincoln's Inn disbarred him 'for conduct unbefitting a barrister and a gentleman'. Hill had complained of his phone being tapped as far back as September 1954. Nobody had taken much notice, but the disbarring of a prominent barrister was an unusual event and the case against Marrinan was based almost entirely on the phone transcripts. Phone tapping aroused considerable controversy and led to the first major crisis faced by the government since Suez. A House of Commons inquiry was set up to investigate the rules and regulations concerning phone tapping and levelled heavy criticism at Home Secretary R. A. B. Butler and his predecessor, Gwilym Lloyd George.

Duncan Webb, as well as continuing to attack the Messinas and their successors, investigated several murder cases and in 1958 provided the police with evidence which secured the acquittal of Ian Gordon, a young airman who had been convicted of the murder of a woman he was courting in Carrickfergus. Because of his youth and good war record he had not been hanged and Webb managed to obtain his release. Webb secured a papal dispensation to marry Cynthia Hume (they were both divorcees) two weeks before he died in September 1958. He was only forty-one years old, but his death was hastened by war wounds rather than underworld enemies. Cynthia's first husband, Donald Hume, was released in February 1958 and immediately confessed to the *Sunday Pictorial* that he really had murdered Stanley Setty. He then left for Switzerland, and in January 1959 murdered a taxi-driver during a bungled robbery. Switzerland had no death penalty and he was sentenced to life imprisonment. After sixteen years in a Swiss prison he was transferred to Broadmoor. Marthe Watts, in retirement after 400 convictions as a common prostitute, attended Webb's funeral. In her memoirs, *The Men in My Life*, she writes of 'my poor friend Duncan, whom I came to know so well' and implies that it was Webb who helped her break free of Gino Messina. Webb's style of crusading journalism was continued by Ken Gardner and Laurie Manifold, culminating in the exposé of Commander Wallace Virgo, who had been taking bribes from pornography dealers for most of the sixties and seventies.

Webb's old enemies the Messinas didn't give up easily, but life for them became much more difficult. In July 1956 Eugenio and Carmelo, who had been sending a steady stream of continental recruits over to England, were tried at Tournai in Belgium for procuring women for the purposes of prostitution. Eugenio was found guilty and given a seven-year sentence. Carmelo was acquitted and told to leave the country within forty-eight hours. By 1959 he was reported to be dying in Sicily. Attilio was arrested in England in 1959 and charged with living off the immoral earnings of Mrs Edna Kallman. He was sentenced to four years' imprisonment and ordered to be deported when he had served his sentence. Alfredo died in Brentford in 1963. Eugenio and Salvatore were still paying rates on Mayfair premises used by prostitutes in 1967.

Superintendent Herbert Sparks, head of the CID at West End Central between 1954 and 1958, went on to become head of the Flying Squad. He retired in 1961 and the following year the *Sunday Pictorial* began serializing his life story. Alfie Hinds, who had been sentenced to twelve years' preventive detention for a robbery at Maples furniture store in Tottenham Court Road in September 1953, sued him for libel. Sparks had written that Hinds was guilty and was lying when he protested otherwise. (Hinds had escaped twice from prison and once from custody at the Law Courts in attempts to publicize his innocence.) The Home Office had stubbornly refused to reopen his case but the *Sunday Pictorial* article allowed Hinds the opportunity he had been waiting for: a chance to persuade a jury that he had been unjustly convicted. As in the Glinski perjury trial, it was a matter of whether or not the jury believed the police evidence. They decided that Sparks had been lying and that Hinds had been framed. He was awarded £1,300 damages and Sparks was ordered to pay the costs of the trial – estimated at £15,000. Hinds was released 'on parole' from Pentonville, where he was serving the last few weeks of his sentence. He died in 1991.

Most of the characters who appear in the early chapters disappeared into obscurity. Kate Meyrick died in the arms of her long-estranged husband in 1932. Darby Sabini, emotionally shattered by the death of his son in the Battle of Britain, moved to Hove, where he operated in a small way as a bookmaker until his death in 1950. Jim Phelan, who wrote so illuminatingly on prison life in the twenties and thirties, became a successful novelist and broadcaster, though he spent much of his later life wandering the by-ways of the English countryside either on foot or in a horse-drawn caravan. Ruby Sparks settled down with a respectable Irish girl and after his last spell in prison swallowed his criminal pride and became an ice-cream salesman. He made enough money to open a newsagent and tobacconist's shop in the Chalk Farm area of London. Eddie Chapman remembers him as a staunch family man with a pleasant wife and happy children. The 'Bobbed-Haired Bandit' was probably already involved with another man when she harboured Ruby in 1940 and very obviously wanted nothing more than to return to respectable anonymity in Wembley Park.

Of Spot's associates, Moisha Blueball involved himself with the Krays when he came out of prison and, according to Spot, 'taught them everything they knew'. They turned out to be ungrateful pupils and he died impoverished and frightened. Sonny the Yank turned his back on crime and put his garrulous talents to good use as a restaurateur. Victor 'Scarface Jock' Russo went back to Coatbridge, near Glasgow, and ran a café. None of Billy Hill's men seemed keen to follow him up there and exact revenge. Parson Basil Andrews settled in Oxford after the perjury trial, where he tried to keep away from drink, gambling and loose women. A newspaper reporter found him living on a church pension of £5 a week and counting every penny. 'Meals must be of the most economical sort. Bread and cheese for lunch. A cheap but hot meal at night. Only very occasionally can he afford a drink.' But after the storm and stress of scandal, he seemed to have found peace at last. Christopher Glinski continued to live on the fringes of the underworld and re-emerged into the limelight as a witness against Frankie Fraser and the Richardson brothers at the 'torture' trial in 1967. In May 1956 Glinski's counsel at the perjury trial, William Rees-Davies, was discovered at a rowdy all-night party dressed in pink pyjamas and surrounded by girls in shortie nighties. It did little to hamper his legal career. Rose Heilbron, Spot's counsel in the Battle of Frith Street trial, became the first woman to be appointed a High Court judge.

After his trials Jack Spot was declared bankrupt and evicted from his flat. As the *Daily Worker* playfully reported in August 1956:

Some of the more censorious neighbours of Mr and Mrs Comer – Jack Spot of Soho fame – have been appealing to their mutual landlord to tip the Comers the black spot by giving them notice to quit their luxury flat in Bayswater. It is just too painful, it seems, for a Queen of the Bridge Tables to have to meet a King of the Underworld in the lift.

Every attempt he made to re-enter the underworld was stamped upon. With the money Rita obtained from selling her life story, she opened the Highball Club, which for a short while was very popular. But Spot's involvement insured that it was plagued by mysterious fires, break-ins and seemingly motiveless vandalism. Hill was taking no chances with his former partner. In the end Spot realized there was no future for him in England, and after being refused admission into Canada, took his family to Ireland. Initially he was treated as a celebrity, but he was happy to lapse into obscurity, making a humble living as a bookie's runner in Dublin and Cork. His marriage survived happily and his daughters grew up and went into show business. After returning to England he never again got into serious trouble and, in the tradition of old East End villains, lived to some extent off his reputation, making occasional appearances at boxing matches and race meetings.

Jack Spot walks down Kensington High Street after being declared bankrupt.

Diary of Criminal Events 1920–60

1920

January   Captain Gerold Fancourt Clayton becomes Deputy Governor of Portland prison.

1921

February   Kate Meyrick opens the 43 Club.
March   Sinn Fein prisoners threaten mutiny at Portland prison.
June   Birmingham mob attacks charabanc full of Leeds bookmakers in mistake for the Sabini mob.

1922

March   Death of Freda Kempton from drug overdose.
April   Captain Clayton becomes Deputy Governor of Pentonville prison.
June   Alexander Paterson appointed to the Prison Commission.
November   Darby and Harry Boy Sabini attacked by the Cortesi brothers in the Fratalanza Club, Great Bath Street.
             (General election: Conservatives 345, Labour 142, Liberals 117.)

1923

June   George Smithson and George Ingram sentenced to long terms of penal servitude for their country house robberies.
December   (General election: Conservatives 258, Labour 191, Liberals 159. Labour forms a minority government.)

1924

February   Jim Phelan sentenced to life imprisonment.
June   George Ingram begins his twenty-two-month hunger strike.
             Cat burglars steal the Wernher jewels from Bath House, Piccadilly.

October	Arrest of 'Brilliant' Chang.
	(General election: Conservatives 419, Labour 151, Liberals 40.)
November	Mrs Meyrick serves her first sentence in Holloway.
December	Arrest of Eddie Manning.

1925

| June | Captain Clayton becomes Governor of Dorchester prison. |

1926

April	Charles 'Bateleur' murdered in the Cochon Club.
May	Percy Sillitoe becomes Chief Constable of Sheffield.
July	Captain Clayton takes over from Captain Stephenson as Governor of Maidstone gaol.

1927

| June | Ruby Sparks arrested and sentenced to three years' penal servitude. |
| September | PC George Gutteridge murdered by Frederick Guy Browne and William Henry Kennedy in a country lane near Stapleford Abbotts, Essex. |

1928

January	Wilfred Macartney sentenced to ten years' penal servitude.
June	Mrs Meyrick sentenced to another six months in Holloway.
September	George Ingram released from Parkhurst.
November	Sergeant Goddard arrested for corruption. Mrs Meyrick rearrested.

1929

April	Captain Clayton takes over from Captain Morgan as Governor of Dartmoor prison.
May	(General election: Labour 288, Conservatives 260, Liberals 59.)
June	Casimir Micheletti and Juan Antonio Castanar deported.
July	George Smithson released from Dartmoor.

1930

| February | Casimir Micheletti murdered by Juan Antonio Castanar in Montmartre. |

May   Ruby Sparks arrested and sentenced to five years' penal servitude to be followed
               by five years' preventive detention.

1931

May   Captain Clayton takes over from Colonel Hales as Governor of Parkhurst prison.
June   Percy Sillitoe becomes Chief Constable of Glasgow.
October   A. N. Roberts takes over from Major Morris as Governor of Dartmoor prison.
               (General election: Victory for Conservative coalition–National Government 521,
               Labour 52, Liberals 33.)

1932

January   Dartmoor mutiny.

1933

February   Death of Mrs Meyrick.
March   Death of Eddie Manning in Parkhurst.

1934

December   Billy Hill released from Wandsworth, marries and carries out a series of smash
               and grab raids.

1935

June   Captain Clayton becomes Governor of Wandsworth prison.
August   Wilfred Macartney released from Parkhurst.
November   (General election: National Government 432, Labour 154.)

1936

January   Murder of Red Max/Emil Allard.
               (George V dies.)
June   Battle of Lewes racecourse.
October   Battle of Cable Street. Jack Spot arrested but gets off with a fine.
               Billy Hill arrested by Inspector Bob Higgins with a cache of furs in Sussex

Gardens, Paddington. After being caught for another robbery while awaiting trial, sentenced to four years' penal servitude in Chelmsford.

November   Darby Sabini declares himself bankrupt.
December   (Edward VIII abdicates.)

1937

May   (Coronation of George VI.)
July   Emergency 999 telephone service introduced.
August   Jim Phelan released after serving over thirteen years' penal servitude.
September   Marthe Huebourg marries sixty-three-year-old drunk, Arthur Watts, and comes to England to work as a prostitute.

1938

June   Jack Spot set upon by Jimmy Wooder, 'Manchester Freddie' and the Islington gang in a Soho billiard hall and badly beaten about the head with billiard cues.
September   Ruby Sparks released from Parkhurst.
               (Munich agreement.)

1939

February   Ruby Sparks arrested and sentenced to five years in Dartmoor.
March   Jack Spot arrested after a fight with blackshirts. Remanded in Brixton prison, where he beats up Antonio Mancini and meets Upton Park gypsy leader Arthur Skurry.
July   Spot takes over a small gambling club in Umberston Street off the Commercial Road. Eddie Chapman arrested in Jersey.
September   (War breaks out.)
               Billy Hill released from Chelmsford.

1940

January   Ruby Sparks escapes from Dartmoor. Recruited by Billy Hill for smash and grab raids. Hill also carries out series of robberies on sub-post offices.
April   Hill caught when escape car stalls following unsuccessful smash and grab raid on jeweller's shop in Conduit Street. Sentenced to two years in Chelmsford.

May   (Churchill replaces Chamberlain as prime minister; German armies invade
                Holland and Belgium; British troops evacuated from Dunkirk.)
June   Ruby Sparks recaptured by Greeno, Higgins and Beveridge.
July   Jack Spot and his gang rounded up by redcaps and drafted into the army.
July/August   (Battle of Britain.)

1941

October   Antonio Mancini hanged for murder of 'Little Hubby' Distelman.
                Albert Dimes bound over for three years.
                Eddie Chapman released from prison in Jersey and becomes a double agent.
December   Billy Hill released from Chelmsford. Returns to robbing post offices. Rents house
                and barn in Bovingdon, Herts., as a run-in for stolen goods.
                (Japanese attack on Pearl Harbor.)

1942

August   Billy Hill chivved by King's Cross hit-man Eddie Raimo.
September   Hill joined by 'Italian Albert' Dimes.
October   Hill's escape car rammed by lorry after attack on Islington postmaster. Sentenced
                to four years in Dartmoor.
November   (British victory at El Alamein.)

1943

July   Jack Spot given a medical discharge.
November   Spot has to leave London after fight with 'Edgware Road Sam'.

1944

February   Ruby Sparks opens the Penguin Club in Soho.
June   (D-Day.)
September   Ruby Sparks arrested for black marketeering.

1945

May   Jack Spot returns to London.
                (VE Day.)

June	Sir Eric Ohlson's Dante wins the Derby: big gambling coup landed by Spot's associates.
July	(General election: Labour majority of 146.)
August	(Atom bombs dropped on Hiroshima and Nagasaki.)
October	Billy Hill comes out of Dartmoor.
	Spot revenges himself on Jimmy Wooder. Re-establishes links with the Upton Park mob.
December	Police try 'dragnet' techniques to halt crime wave – road blocks, closing bridges, etc.

1946

January	Ghost Squad formed, headed by 'Charlie Artful' Capstick.
	Jack Spot managing gambling club in St Botolph's Lane.

1947

January	Jack Spot's feud with the Whites reaches climax: fight with Johnny Warren in Soho pub leads to 'Battle of Sackville Street'. Spot goes to Southend until things quieten down.
April	Alec de Antiquis shot after a bungled jeweller's shop robbery in Charlotte Street. Police, led by Robert Fabian and Bob Higgins, begin a vigorous clamp-down on the underworld.
	Archie Hill attempts to beat up Victor 'Scarface Jock' Russo but gets more than he bargained for.
July	Eugenio Messina and Charles Vassalo arrested after incriminating each other in struggle for power. According to Arthur Helliwell: 'With the rival tsars of vice safely behind bars and a £1,000 a week business there for the snatching, plots are being hatched faster than eggs on a poultry farm' (but he underestimated the power of the Messinas).
August	Billy Hill arrested on a warehouse-breaking charge. Flees to South Africa. Opens the Club Millionaire in Johannesburg. Fight with underworld boss Arnold Neville leads to arrest.
September	Hill returns to London and hides out in East Ham.
	Financial crisis leads to petrol rationing and abolition of foreign travel allowance. Society people prosecuted for currency smuggling and dealings with 'Black Max' Intrator.
October	Hill carries out robbery in Manchester with Sammy Josephs/Ross and while up

there falls in love with a night-club hostess. Decides to give himself up and face warehouse-breaking charge. Sentenced to three years in Wandsworth.

November   (Marriage between Princess Elizabeth and Philip Mountbatten.)

1948

January   Criminal Justice Act abolishes hard labour, penal servitude and flogging and brings in new provisions for preventive detention.

March   Georgie Sinden tries to shoot Jack Spot in the Apex Club, Mile End.
(British withdraw from Palestine.)

July   Attempted robbery at Heathrow Airport foiled by police ambush led by Bob Lee and Bill 'the Cherub' Chapman.
(National Health Service inaugurated.)
(Olympic Games held in London.)

August   Spot forced to close St Botolph's Lane club because of links with airport robbery.

November/   Lynskey Tribunal investigates 'contact man' Sidney Stanley's links with govern-
December   ment ministers.

1949

October   Headless torso of second-hand car dealer 'Big Stan' Setty found in Essex marshes. Donald Hume arrested for murder. Duncan Webb befriends his wife and later marries her.

November   Jack Spot meets Billy Hill on his release from prison and provides him with new clothes and furniture.

1950

February   Billy Hill cuts 'Jack Delight' (Jackie Sangers) to ribbons; Jack Spot has to straighten things out. Spot goes to Paris to meet Ralph Capone and Frankie Garbo and persuades them to keep out of British boxing.

June   (North Koreans invade South Korea.)

July   (General Election: Labour majority down to five.)

September   Duncan Webb's Messina exposé.

October   Darby Sabini dies in his bed in Hove.

November   Hill and Spot open club in Southend, relying on Jackie Reynolds and Teddy Machin to run it for them.

1951

March	Jack Spot meets future wife at Haydock Park races.
May	Billy Hill takes over Trafalgar Square photography racket – threatening to put green dye in the fountains and poison the pigeons with cyanide peas in order to oust the local boss.
	(Festival of Britain.)
June	Hill runs club for Spot in Berwick Street. Begins associating with Gypsy Riley, who looks after the bar.
	(Burgess and Maclean defect to Moscow.)
July	Hill and Spot open posh spieler opposite the Windmill in Ham Yard, with financial backing from old villain 'Freddy Ford'.
August	Hill and Spot stop feuding between (Mad Frankie) Fraser gang and (Johnnie) Carter gang in south London.
	Hill and Spot stop dog-racing feud between Ginger Rumble's mob and the remnants of the White mob.
	Hill slashes Belgian Johnny because of insult to Gypsy. Spot has to straighten things out.
September	Hill goes to the south of France with Gypsy, Spot, Rita and Patsy 'Golden Hands' Murphy.
October	Rita gets pregnant and marries Spot.
	Spot goes to see Arthur Helliwell at the *People* to announce his retirement.
	(General election: Tory majority of 17.)

1952

February	(Death of George VI.)
May	Mailbag robbery in Eastcastle Street – £287,000 stolen.
June	Billy Hill buys into the toy business; opens legitimate drinking clubs – one of them (the New Cabinet Club) run by his wife, Aggie; claims financial stakes in bookmaking enterprises: helps various mobs get rid of gear.
July	Jack Spot and Rita's first daughter born.
October	Aggie leaves Hill because of involvement with Gypsy. He buys her a poodle (Chico) and lets her keep the club. Hill goes on holiday to Casablanca, Marrakesh, Algiers, Monte Carlo, Tangier and Gibraltar.
	Teddy Machin, Big Jim Tibbs and four others accused of causing a disturbance at the Madeleine Members Club, South Molton Street, Mayfair.

1953

March	Police arrest Black Bess and smash the Red Scarf gang. (Death of Stalin.)
June	(Coronation of Elizabeth II.)
July	Billy Hill arranges for Sir Gordon Richards's stolen jewellery to be returned to him.
August	Slip Sullivan, one of Hill's croupiers, beats up Maltese pimp (Tulip) and is slashed by his minder 'Brownson' (Tommy Smithson).
September	Smithson badly cut up by Hill round the back of the Black Cat Cigarette factory in Camden Town. Jack Spot has to straighten things out. Sullivan sent down for twenty-one months.
	Spot arrested in a West End telephone box by Detective Sergeant Careless. Accused of possessing an offensive weapon. Let off with a fine and a warning.
December	Freddy Andrews, childhood associate of Hill's, chivved. Hill charged with grievous bodily harm.

1954

February	Billy Hill acquitted on GBH charge when Freddy Andrews refuses to identify him as one of the attackers.
March	Hill and Eddie Chapman sail to Tangier on *The Flamingo*. Jack Spot refuses to get involved and opens a drinking club in Old Compton Street.
April	Some of the airport robbers, including Georgie Woods, released.
June	Hill involved in plot to kidnap Sultan of Morocco from imprisonment in Madagascar.
July	*The Flamingo* sails to Savona, Corsica and Toulon – where it catches fire. Hill and crew return to London.
September	£45,000-worth of gold bullion hijacked from KLM van in Jockey's Fields, Holborn. Guy Mahon, head of Flying Squad, and Bob Lee, recently moved from head of Flying Squad to head of No. 3 District, work together on the case.
	'The Amazing Confessions of Billy Hill' begin in the *People*.
	Hill's East End toy factory turned over by the police.
October	Spot beats up Duncan Webb.

1955

January	Jack Spot's story appears in the *Sunday Chronicle* – both Billy Hill and Spot have now publicly declared themselves 'Boss of the Underworld' and 'King of Soho'.
	Slip Sullivan murdered – big funeral.

April	Hill sails to Australia with Gypsy.
May	(General Election: Tory majority of 60.)
June	Hill and Gypsy return from Australia, having been refused entry.
July	Execution of Ruth Ellis.
	Death of Bill 'the Cherub' Chapman, who had led police operations at Heathrow in 1948.
August	Worsening relations between Spot and the Italian bookies erupts into violence when Spot attempts to teach Albert Dimes a lesson in Frith Street.
September	Duncan Webb exposes 'the wickedest man in the world', Lucky Luciano, and his world-wide dope racket.
	Elderly clergyman Basil Andrews and Croix de Guerre holder Christopher Glinski persuade jury to aquit Spot of attack on Dimes.
	Webb prints his exposé of 'the Knocking Parson' in the *People*.
	Glinski arrested for perjury.
	(Commercial television begins.)
October	Moisha Blueball (Morris Goldstein), Sonny the Yank (Bernard Schach) and Rita arrested for conspiracy to commit perjury.
November	Grech/Hannam/Canter police corruption trial.
	Duncan Webb exposes 'Britain's biggest vice boss' – Maurice Conley.
	Basil Andrews perjury trial – he incriminates his fellow conspirators.
	Party at Gennaro's restaurant, Soho, to celebrate the publication of Hill's book, *Boss of Britain's Underworld*.
December	Glinski found not guilty of perjury despite police evidence.

1956

March	Duncan Webb wins £732 costs and damages in a civil action against Jack Spot for attack of October 1954.
May	Eugenio Messina found guilty of white slavery charges at Tournai, Belgium; Carmelo acquitted but deported.
	Spot and Rita attacked near their Hyde Park Mansions home. He needs seventy-eight stitches and a blood transfusion.
	Bobbie Warren and Frankie Fraser arrested for the attack on Spot.
	Frett, Rosa and Frankie Fraser charged with GBH against Johnnie Carter (Fraser not brought to trial).
June	Warren and Fraser sentenced to seven years each for attack on Spot.
	Frett and Rosa sentenced to seven years each for attack on Carter. Judge warns of gang warfare.

Tommy 'Bonz' Falco slashed outside Astor Club in Berkeley Square.

Tommy Smithson murdered by Maltese pimps – 'he was as harmless as a day-old chick' (Sammy Samuels).

July	Tommy Smithson's funeral.
	Spot tried for Falco slashing and found not guilty.
	Report that Billy Hill was beaten up by rival gangster – possibly Billy Howard, the governor of south London.
August	Hanging abolished.
	Arrest of 'Little Billy' Blythe, 'Battles' Rossi and 'Ginger' Dennis for attack on Spot.
September	Webb starts another Messina exposé.
October	Blythe sentenced to five years, Dennis and Rossi to four each, for attack on Spot.
November	(Suez Crisis – British, French and Israeli forces invade Egypt.)
	(Russians invade Hungary.)

1957

January	(Macmillan succeeds Eden as prime minister.)
February	Billy Blythe dies in prison: big funeral at Kensal Green cemetery.
	Jack Spot declared bankrupt.
March	Gypsy charged with gouging out a man's eye.
May	Johnny Rice jailed for twelve months.
July	Patrick Marrinan disbarred.
	Spot, Rita and children evicted from Hyde Park Mansions.
September	Spot goes to Canada but is not allowed in.
October	(Russians launch Sputnik 1.)

1958

January	Jack Spot discharged from bankruptcy.
February	Donald Hume released from prison. Confesses to the *Sunday Pictorial* that he did murder Stanley Setty.
March	(First CND Aldermaston March.)
June	Spot and Rita open the Highball Club in Lancaster Gate.
July	Twenty men with crowbars pay a visit to the Highball Club.
August	Highball Club burnt down. Spot and Rita go to Ireland.
	(Notting Hill riots.)
September	Duncan Webb marries Cynthia Hume shortly before dying of leukaemia.

1959

March	Lady Docker asks Billy Hill to recover her jewels.
June	Hill goes into the antiques business.
August	Hill beats up professional gambler Joe Wade at the Star, Belgravia.
October	(General election: Tory majority of 100.)

1960

February	Selwyn Cooney, manager of Aggie Hill's New Cabinet club, murdered by Jimmy Nash in the Pen Club, Duval Street, Whitechapel, which was run by Tommy Smithson's ex-girlfriend Fay Salder.
July	Betting and Gaming Bill to legalize off-course gambling passes through Parliament.
	Death of Brenda Dean Paul.

Further Reading

Many of these books are long out of print, but in their day they were very popular and they can often be picked up in second-hand bookshops. Films too are a useful source. British cinema never developed a gangster genre and British crime films – from *Blackmail* to *The Sweeney* – have tended to look at crime from the policeman's point of view. This doesn't mean they show no insight into the workings of the underworld. Ken Annakin's *The Informers* (1963) and David Greene's *The Strange Affair* (1968) are both convincing in what they show of interaction between crooks and the police. John Boulting's film *Brighton Rock* (1947) has some frightening sequences of racetrack violence, and Val Guest's *Hell Is a City* (1960) depicts a raid on an authentic-looking tossing ring somewhere between Manchester and Sheffield. Though most British crime films embody a conformist law and order ethos, this is sometimes subverted by charismatic villains who win our sympathy despite their misdeeds. The spivs played by Stewart Granger in *Waterloo Road* (1945), Griffith Jones in *They Made Me a Fugitive* (1947) and *Good Time Girl* (1948), Bill Owen in *Dancing with Crime* (1947), Michael Medwin in *Black Memory* (1947), Nigel Patrick in *Noose* (1948) and Richard Widmark in *Night and the City* (1950) are too sharp and clever not to command a degree of respect. And the flashy underworld professionals played by Stanley Baker in *The Criminal* (1960), Tom Bell in *He Who Rides a Tiger* (1965) and Michael Caine in *Get Carter* (1971) are heroes as well as villains. If one wants to dig deeper, then it is necessary to talk to policemen and criminals, many of whom are wonderful story-tellers.

Barr, Robert, *The Scotland Yard Story*, Hodder & Stoughton, 1962

Bean, J. P., *The Sheffield Gang Wars*, D. & D. Publications, Sheffield, 1981

Benney, Mark (Henry Ernest Degras), *Low Company*, Peter Davies, 1936

—— 'The Truth about English Prisons', *Fact*, no. 12, 1938

—— *Gaol Delivery*, Longmans Green, 1948

Berrett, James, *When I Was at Scotland Yard*, Sampson, Low, Marston, 1932

Beveridge, Peter, *Inside the C.I.D.*, Evan Brothers, 1957

Browne, Eddie, *Road Pirate*, John Long, 1934

Burke, Shifty (Peggy Benton), *Peterman*, Arthur Barker, 1966

Cannon, Joe, *Tough Guys Don't Cry*, Magnus, 1983

Capstick, John, *Given in Evidence*, John Long, 1960

Cartwright, Frederick, *G-Men of the GPO*, Sampson, Low, Marston, 1937

Champly, Henri, *The Road to Shanghai*, John Long, 1934

Chapman, Eddie, *The Real Eddie Chapman Story*, Library 33, 1966

Chesney, Kellow, *The Victorian Underworld*, Penguin, 1970

Chibnall, Steve, *Law and Order News*, Tavistock, 1977

Clayton, Gerold Fancourt, *The Wall Is Strong*, John Long, 1958

Cousins, Sheila, *To Beg I Am Ashamed*, George Routledge, 1938

Croft-Cooke, Rupert, *Smiling Damned Villain*, Secker & Warburg, 1959

Crookston, Peter, *Villain*, Jonathan Cape, 1967

Davis, Val, *Gentlemen of the Broad Arrows*, Selwyn & Blount, 1935

Dendrickson, George and Thomas, Frederick, *The Truth about Dartmoor*, Victor Gollancz, 1954

Dey, T. H., *Leaves from a Bookmaker's Book*, Hutchinson, 1930

Divall, Tom, *Scoundrels and Scalliwags*, Ernest Benn, 1929

Du Parcq, Herbert, *Report on the Circumstances Connected with the Recent Disorder at Dartmoor Convict Prison*, HMSO, 1932

Du Rose, John, *Murder Was My Business*, Mayflower, 1973

Endle, Rufus, *Dartmoor Prison*, Bossiney Books, 1979

Fabian, Robert, *Fabian of the Yard*, Naldrett Press, 1950

—— *London after Dark*, Naldrett Press, 1954

Felstead, S. Theodore, *The Underworld of London*, John Murray, 1923

—— *Strange Company*, Hutchinson, 1930

Ferrier, J. K., *Crooks and Crime*, Seeley, Service, 1928

Firmin, Stanley, *Scotland Yard: The Inside Story*, Hutchinson, 1948

—— *Men in the Shadows*, Hutchinson, 1953

Fordham, Peta, *Inside the Underworld*, Allen & Unwin, 1972

Frost, George 'Jack', *Flying Squad*, Youth Book Club, 1950

Furneaux, Rupert, *Famous Criminal Cases*, vol. 3, Allan Wingate, 1956

Gallacher, William, *The Last Memoirs of William Gallacher*, Lawrence & Wishart, 1966

Gosling, John, *The Ghost Squad*, W. H. Allen, 1959

—— and Warner, Douglas, *The Shame of a City*, W. H. Allen, 1960

Graves, Robert and Hodge, Alan, *The Long Weekend*, Faber & Faber, 1940

Greeno, Edward, *War on the Underworld*, John Long, 1960

Higgins, Robert, *In the Name of the Law*, John Long, 1958

Hill, Billy, *Boss of Britain's Underworld*, Naldrett Press, 1955

Hinds, Alfred, *Contempt of Court*, Bodley Head, 1966

Hogg, Garry, *Safe Bind, Safe Find*, Phoenix House, 1961

Horler, Sidney, *London's Underworld*, Hutchinson, 1934

Howe, Sir Ronald, *The Pursuit of Crime*, Arthur Barker, 1961

Howgrave-Graham, H. M., *Light and Shade at Scotland Yard*, John Murray, 1947

Hughes, David, 'The Spivs', in Philip French and Michael Sissons (eds.), *The Age of Austerity*, Hodder & Stoughton, 1963

Hughes, Robert, *The Fatal Shore*, Pan, 1988

Ingram, George and Mackenzie, De Witt, *Hell's Kitchen*, Herbert Jenkins, 1930

Jackson, Sir Richard, *Occupied with Crime*, George Harrap, 1967

Janson, Hank (Stephen D. Frances), *Jack Spot: Man of a Thousand Cuts*, Alexander Moring, 1959

Kellard, Gilbert, *Crime in London*, Grafton, 1987

Lucas, Netley, *Crooks: Confessions*, Hurst & Blackwell, 1925

Lucas, Norman, *Britain's Gangland*, W. H. Allen, 1969

—— and Scarlett, Bernard, *The Flying Squad*, Arthur Barker, 1968

Macartney, Wilfred, *Walls Have Mouths*, Victor Gollancz, 1936

McConnell, Brian, *The Evil Firm*, Mayflower, 1969

McKibbin, Ross, 'Working-Class Gambling in Britain 1880–1939', *Past and Present*, no. 82, 1979

Mannheim, H., *War and Crime*, Watt & Co., 1941

Mark, Sir Robert, *In the Office of Constable*, Collins, 1978

Merrow Smith, L. W. and Harris, James, *Prison Screw*, Herbert Jenkins, 1962

Meyrick, Kate, *Secrets of the 43*, John Long, 1933

Mortimer, Roger, *The Jockey Club*, Cassell, 1958

Norman, Frank, *Bang to Rights*, Secker & Warburg, 1958

Owen, Frank, *The Eddie Chapman Story*, Allan Wingate, 1953

—— *Free Agent: The Further Adventures of Eddie Chapman*, Allan Wingate, 1955

Parker, Robert, *Rough Justice*, Fontana, 1981

Parr, Eric, *Grafters All*, Max Reinhardt, 1964

Paul, Brenda Dean, *My First Life*, John Long, 1934

Payne, Leslie, *The Brotherhood*, Michael Joseph, 1973

Pearson, John, *The Profession of Violence*, Weidenfeld & Nicolson, 1972

Phelan, Jim, *Jail Journey*, Secker & Warburg, 1940

—— *The Underworld*, George Harrap, 1953

—— *Criminals in Real Life*, Burke, 1956

—— *Fetters for Twenty*, Burke, 1957

—— *Nine Murderers and Me*, Phoenix House, 1967

—— *Meet the Criminal Classes*, Tallis Press, 1969

Priestley, Philip, *Jail Journeys*, Routledge, 1989

Proctor, Harry, *The Street of Disillusion*, Allan Wingate, 1958

Progl, Zoe, *Woman of the Underworld*, Arthur Barker, 1964

Raven, Charles, *Underworld Nights*, Hulton Press, 1956

Read, Leonard, with Morton, James, *Nipper*, Warner, 1992

Richmond, Guy, *Prison Doctor*, Nunaga, 1975

Ruggles-Brise, Sir Evelyn, *The English Prison System*, Macmillan, 1921

Samuel, Raphael, *East End Underworld*, Routledge & Kegan Paul, 1981

Samuels, Sammy and Davis, Leonard, *Among the Soho Sinners*, Robert Hale, 1970

Scott, Sir Harold, *Scotland Yard*, Andre Deutsch, 1954

Sharpe, F. D., *Sharpe of the Flying Squad*, John Long, 1938

Sillitoe, Sir Percy, *Cloak without Dagger*, Cassell, 1955

Smithies, Edward, *Crime in Wartime*, Allen & Unwin, 1982

—— *The Black Economy in England since 1914*, Gill & Macmillan, Dublin, 1984

Smithson, George, *Raffles in Real Life*, Hutchinson, 1930

Sparks, Herbert, *Iron Man*, John Long, 1964

Sparks, Ruby and Price, Norman, *Burglar to the Nobility*, Arthur Barker, 1961

Sparrow, Judge Gerald, *Gang-Warfare*, Feature Books, 1968

Spencer, John C., *Crime in the Services*, Routledge & Kegan Paul, 1954

Stedman Jones, Gareth, *Outcast London*, Penguin, 1984

Taylor, A. J. P., *English History 1914–1945*, Penguin, 1970

Thorp, Arthur, *Calling Scotland Yard*, Allan Wingate, 1954

Tietjen, Arthur, *Soho: London's Vicious Circle*, Allan Wingate, 1956

Totterdell, G. H., *Country Copper*, George Harrap, 1956

Tullett, Tom, *Inside Dartmoor*, Frederick Muller, 1966

Vamplew, Wray, *The Turf*, Allen Lane, 1976

Walsh, Dermot, *Break-Ins*, Constable, 1980

Watts, Marthe, *The Men in My Life*, Christopher Johnson, 1960

Webb, Duncan, *Crime Is My Business*, Frederick Muller, 1953

—— *Deadline for Crime*, Frederick Muller, 1955

—— *Line Up for Crime*, Frederick Muller, 1956

Whitcomb, J. F., *The Trial of Alfredo Messina*, WLA, 1952

Wickstead, Bert, *Gangbuster*, Futura, 1985

Wilkinson, Laurence, *Behind the Face of Crime*, Frederick Muller, 1957

Wood, Stuart, *Shades of the Prison House*, Williams & Norgate, 1932

Worby, John, *The Other Half*, J. M. Dent, 1937

—— *Spiv's Progress*, J. M. Dent, 1939

Glossary

This is only a small selection of underworld jargon and doesn't include many examples of back slang (the kaycab jinnals) or of the much more common – and ever changing – rhyming slang; and I have ignored words which have passed into common parlance (bogey, bottle, iffy, etc.).

bang to rights caught red-handed, with no hope of pleading innocence

bang up to lock in a cell

bird prison sentence (*bird lime* = time)

blag wage snatching, robbery with violence

brass prostitute

broadsman cardsharper

burnt window (*burnt cinder* = winder; *stiff burnt* = plate-glass window)

busy detective

buyer receiver of stolen goods

buzz steal as a pickpocket (working on one's own); see also *whizz*

cane (*peter cane*) jemmy

carpet three-month prison sentence

case check out (generally premises prior to burglary)

chisel swindle

chiv a taped-up razor with only an inch or so of blade showing, used for cutting and slashing, not for stabbing

chokey punishment cells

climber cat burglar

cop receive (*cop a drop* = accept a bribe)

cozzer policeman

daily improbable story (*Daily Mail* = tall tale); cf. *ship* (ship under sail) and *Binnie* (Binnie Hale, a famous thirties actress)

dairy-take to distract attention while some illicit action is perpetrated

diddikoi gypsy, or, more exactly, a half-gypsy

drag (noun) a motor vehicle, (verb) to steal from cars; also fairground slang for the road

drum a flat or house; also a tin carried by a tramp in which to cook food and make tea

factory police station

flatty policeman in uniform

flowery cell (*flowery dell*)

godforbids (kids) children, extended to offence of sexual interference with children

grass an informer/to inform

groin ring (with stones)

guv'nor senior policeman/gang boss

hairy rape (*hairy ape*)

have one's collar felt to be arrested

hoister shoplifter

hook thief

hooting and hollering making a lot of noise about nothing

iron homosexual, generally male prostitute (*iron-hoof* = poof)

jargoons convincing but worthless artificial stones

judas peep-hole in cell door

jump up stealing from lorries

kite cheque

knockers and tappers scroungers and cadgers

lagging three years' penal servitude/any substantial prison sentence

line-up identity parade

lolly-popped informed against

lumber prostitute's term for what she does with clients

madam lying or misleading story

manor the territory of a particular criminal or police officer

minder bodyguard/troubleshooter

Mr Wood policeman's truncheon

monkey £500

mystery a poor, generally homeless, girl, open to exploitation

narkit watch out!

peter prison, police cell or safe

peterman safebreaker

piker unreliable person (sometimes applied to gypsies)

pipe watch

ponce pimp, *souteneur*, man who lives on a prostitute's earnings

pony £25

pussy furs or cat-o'-nine-tails

red gold

rubber drinking or gambling club (*rubber-dub-dub* = club)

run-in secret location for unloading and sometimes storing stolen goods

screaming informing or confessing to the police

screw (noun) prison officer, (verb) to break into houses or safes

screwsman burglar or safe-breaker

slag small time/contemptible crooks

slaughter dividing up the spoils of a robbery

slop a policeman

smiler long-term convict with a good store of tobacco

snide counterfeit

snout informer/tobacco

spieler gambling club

squarehead not very bright provincial criminal

steamer law-abiding, rule-obeying person (*steamer tug* = mug)

stick jemmy

stir prison

stoppo escape

strawberries and cream bread and water punishment

strength information, facts

stretch one-year prison sentence

stripe cutting someone's face with a chiv

swallow to accept a situation without protest

swede not very bright provincial criminal

talking in telephone numbers   wildly exaggerating the figures involved in past or projected robberies and frauds

tealeaf   thief

team   fairly regular gang of criminals

tearaway   small-time but generally violent and reckless criminal

tom   prostitute

tomfoolery   jewellery

tooled up   to be equipped with weapons or tools necessary for carrying out a crime

turned over   premises raided by the police, whether home, run-in or prison cell

tweedle   theft of jewellery by substituting artificial for real stones

twirl   key or prison warder

verbals   report of 'off the record' (and often self-incriminatory) remarks made by a suspect on being arrested

villain   a crook of some standing

weigh off   to sentence

whizz   picking pockets (as a team)

wide   aware of how the world works, of the codes of the underworld

workman   someone employed in a drinking club or spieler

Index

Page numbers in italics refer to illustrations.